CASES IN CONSUMER BEHAVIOR

CASES IN CONSUMER BEHAVIOR

Volume I

Martha McEnally

Upper Saddle River, New Jersey 07458

Acquisitions editor: Whitney Blake
Assistant editor: Anthony Palmiotto
Production editor: Carol Zaino
Manufacturer: Victor Graphics

ISBN 0-13-066558-4

10 9 8 7 6 5 4 3 2

CONTENTS

This book is dedicated to one who always helps me keep my perspective and is my major source of inspiration -- Dr. B. A. Bobb.

Changing Consumer Perceptions of Bud Riley's

The Wife's Dilemma:

Dana had gotten home early from work and was planning to make a start on a summer tan by stretching out on the patio when Nick burst through the door, yelling "Hey Hon, let's go to the store and look at DVDs." Joe, (Sam's work partner) had gotten a DVD and, since then, that was all that Dana had heard. "I really want to lie in the sun – it's such a great spring afternoon. And besides, I have a million other things to do," Dana said while thinking, "I can't stand going shopping for electronics with Nick. He looks and looks and he and the sales guys are busy yakking about tracking systems, megabytes, or whatever. It's so boring."

"But there are sales on everywhere, so now's the time to look for a new system. We've had that VCR for six years; the pictures are faded; we can get digital sound *and* you'll be able to see Brad Pitt more clearly…What'cha say?…It won't take long." Thinking fast, Nick added, "We could eat out."

"I hate, hate, hate this. He'll go on for hours, if we don't go. Boys and their toys is right!" Dana thought. "We will have to replace the VCR, but does it have to be today? I hate going to those stores…I wish …"

How is Dana going to finish that thought?

The Advertising Problem:

Elsewhere, Chris Carlson, account executive at Trone Advertising, had just left a tumultuous meeting with the marketing research and advertising team for the Riley's account – a regional chain of electronics stores. They had spent several hours discussing the results of Riley's marketing research. Although Chris had worked with Riley's for only a year, the account had provided many challenges.

At present, Skip Bowen, owner of Riley's, wanted to improve the chain's image through re-positioning. To do that, he had agreed to a marketing research project to determine possible new positioning strategies and was quite anxious to see what ideas Chris and his team had come up with based on the research. However, the team couldn't agree and Chris was running out of time.

"We've got to come up with a slam-dunk idea soon," he thought. "I've got a client who wants exciting, new image advertising and we can't agree on how to position the firm." Highly frustrated, Chris decided to call it quits for the day and to spend some time in one of the stores observing customers.

On his way to the store, he began to review the advertising that he had already done for Riley's, hoping it would inspire him with a winning idea for re-positioning the firm – an idea that he could use as the theme of the next major advertising campaign. Chris was sure that the key to improving the chain's profit picture was changing consumer perceptions of the stores. That meant re-positioning the store. "We have got to make changes and get customers in the store – and soon," he thought as he pulled into the parking lot.

The Advertiser: Riley's Inc.

Riley's actually began life as Bud Riley's. The first store opened in the late 1940s, offering appliances to consumers who desperately needed to update their pre-World War II appliances. Sales received another big boost in the1950s and 1960s thanks to a new invention – television. Times were good and Bud Riley's expanded to over twenty in-state locations, thereby greatly increasing sales and profitability. One factor enabling Bud Riley's to expand was the lack of competition. Of course, there was Sears, but it was not really pushing electronics at that time.

In the '70s, the competitive picture changed. Circuit City, a large specialty retailer of appliances and electronics products, opened stores in several cities in the state. It had two major advantages over Bud Riley's: lower prices due to greater buying power and volume, and a wider selection made possible by larger stores. Circuit City is called a category killer because it carries all the popular models of major electronics and appliances products. Whatever most consumers want can be found in one of their stores.

The nature of the consumer market changed along with competitive changes. The sales surge of the late 1940s based on pent-up demand was a matter of replacing old appliances. But by the 50s, households were upgrading by acquiring "new" appliances such as dryers, televisions, and frost-free refrigerators for the first time. Effective selling meant educating consumers about the features of these new products. Consumers needed to know about options, benefits and financing. Banks helped by pushing low interest loans that enabled Americans to trade up to more expensive brands.

By the 1960s, appliances had reached the maturity stage of the product life cycle. Hence, to push product, retailers used heavy promotional efforts and price competition became standard in the industry. Because lots of merchandise had to be moved through each retail location, stores got larger and larger enabling consumers to comparison shop for hours. To cut costs, the role of the salesperson was reduced, which fit in with a strategy of offering only popular products that had already reached the latter part of the product life cycle growth stage. By that time, consumers were familiar with the product and didn't require as many sales people. Thus, category killer operations did not introduce new products such as home computers until the market was familiar with them; instead specialty stores performed that function. This gave small chains like Bud Riley's a chance for survival. They could introduce new products that sold at wider margins because they had the needed sales help. They kept the appliances because it was expected of them and helped to build sales volumes and revenues. Thus Bud Riley's used a combination strategy of low margins/high volume (appliances) and high margin/low volume (computers) because it used their sales staff to build competitive advantage.

The decade of the '80s brought even more competition from discounters such as Wal-Mart and Sam's. While these two retailers did not have the selection advantage that Circuit City did, they were formidable competitors on pricing – as both were fond of saying "Always the lowest price." By now, televisions and appliances were commodity items traded on the basis of price so that retailers such as Wal-Mart and Sam's could successfully sell these items on a self service basis. Because Sam's and Wal-Mart sold mostly basic washers and appliances, customers had to seek out stores such as Circuit City, Sears or a specialty store such as Bud Riley's for products that had more features or for in-store sales help in customizing their stereo systems.

In spite of reliance on the combination strategy, Bud Riley's began losing money in the late 1980s – a trend that continued into the nineties. The strategy of boosting sales with new products did not seem to be working so well. And then, two new products appeared on the horizon – DVDs and High Definition TV (HDTV).

Industry observers expected that the widespread availability of HDTV would start a new product life cycle in which households would spend thousands upgrading not only their television, but also their stereo systems. The result would be theater quality entertainment available in the consumer's own living room. With the addition of interactive cable television systems, the consumers could access the Internet to watch major movies with digital sound at any time, create their own concerts, shop, and do a myriad of other activities. The profits to be made with these systems could be tremendous and offer specialty chains like Riley's an opportunity to regain its profitability – at least until HDTV reached the maturity stage of the product life cycle.

To take advantage of the opportunity that HDTV offered, Skip Bowen hired a new, more sophisticated management team, Dave Lattimore and Sam Osborne. Both of them had significant retailing experience and realized right away that the current advertising strategy had to change. Past management had held the line on advertising costs by using the lowest cost media to promote sales. To completely turn the advertising around, they decided to start over with a new ad agency – Trone Advertising of High Point, North Carolina.

In line with a fresh advertising start, Dave and Sam made a number of changes to improve consumers' image of the chain. First, they changed the name from Bud Riley's to Riley's and commissioned a new logo. Second, they began renovating stores to make them more modern, less crowded-looking and more attractive. Third, they hired sales trainers to work with the sales people to teach them techniques other than the high-pressure ones that they had used in the past. In line with the renovation of the stores, they gave the sales people polo shirts with the new logo. By eliminating the traditional suits and ties, they hoped to create a more relaxed atmosphere and distance themselves from Circuit City's salesmen in suits.

The Agency: Trone Advertising

Trone Advertising was founded on April Fool's Day in 1982 when Lee Trone, Bob Donohoe and Jim Johnson left their previous employer. It was a true start-up operation with no clients, no billings and no income. Five years later, Donohoe and Johnson had departed – in part because they were not as driven as Lee Trone – but the firm lacked a major client. Then, representatives from R. J. Reynolds approached Trone to design a campaign to celebrate the 75th anniversary of Camel cigarettes. The result was the birth of Joe Camel – probably the best known and possibly one of the most controversial of advertising cartoon creations. Trone's success with the Reynolds account brought them other clients. By the late 1990s, Trone Advertising employed more than 100 people and had billings of over $70 million which placed them nineteenth among southeastern advertising agencies, according to <u>Adweek</u> magazine.

Trone is known for its hip – sometimes sassy – advertising. It can be a little irreverent and attention-getting or it can create highly polished sophisticated ads. Besides Joe Camel, they have given us such snazzy slogans as "When America parties, it Cooks" for Cook's champagne. For a local brand, Stanback Headache Powders, it created television commercials in which fast-talking characters use such cliches as "zip," "hot-footin'," "scoot," "scram," and "skedaddle" to describe how quickly Stanback cures a headache. The agency also has created sophisticated advertising for clients such as Jefferson Pilot Insurance. For all clients, Trone delivers a quality, up-to-date product backed by careful market research and highly creative advertising efforts.

Chris Carlson, who was a relative newcomer to Trone as he had been there only 4 years, led the Riley's account. When assigned to the account, Chris' original reaction can be summed up in one word: Panic! He realized that the workload on this account would be heavy because retailers run so many ads. His team would be constantly trying to think of different ways to say "sale." To add to Chris' frustration, he had very little experience with retail advertising.

The First Newspaper Campaign: Death toZorro and a Restoration of Taste

The first request that Dave and Sam made to Chris was for new newspaper ads – to run within a week! When Chris looked at recent advertising for Bud Riley's, he was appalled. The ads featured dozens of items that completely filled the page, producing a very cluttered, busy look. Because there was little white space, they were hard to read. Worse yet, some of them used movie characters of the past such as Godzilla who crushed prices and Zorro who slashed prices. These ads left consumer's with the impression that there was a barrel-bellied, cigar smokin', good ole' boy named Bud Riley who owned the stores which was definitely not the image that Dave and Sam wanted. By eliminating the name, Bud, from the chain's name, they hoped to overcome that image.

To support a more sophisticated image, the creative team immediately developed ads that featured fewer items, had more white space, eliminated Godzilla and Zorro, and in general had a more tasteful appearance. Because Trone management believes in on-going research, they asked local store managers to fax them evaluations of these ads and their impact in local markets. Besides gathering opinions of the new advertising, the faxed comments enabled Chris to determine which products to advertise, the best days to run ads and the amount of store traffic generated by the ads. In general, the comments were positive and enthusiastic – the new look sold well with managers and customers.

But Chris and his team realized that much more research and work would be necessary to turn around the old Bud Riley's image. With the help of Doug Barton, Trone's director of marketing research, they conducted two focus groups in order to understand the market better. Specifically they wanted to know:

- the shopping habits of customers, i.e. where they shop and their reasons for purchase
- how consumers thought of the shopping experience, i.e. was it enjoyable or painful?
- their images of electronics stores (Bud Riley's, Circuit City and Sears)
- what attributes an ideal store would have
- the consumers' exposure to and experience with home theater.

The focus groups met on a Sunday afternoon in a renovated Riley's store in one of the state's major cities. Participants were screened to meet the following criteria: they had to be 25-49 years old, to have minimum incomes of $25,000 for singles and $30,000 for couples, to be the primary or equal decision maker in an electronics purchase, and to have purchased an electronic product (TV, VCR/DVD, Stereo Equipment or Camcorder) in the last twelve months *or* to be planning to buy such a product in the next six months. In every group, there should be at least four individuals with an income of $45,000 or more. By including some higher income individuals, the focus groups more closely resembled the local market. The researchers decided that one group should be female and the other male because each gender has different buying motivations.

The results of the focus groups are summarized in Exhibit 1. Although this research provided a large amount of information, the results did not pinpoint specific problem areas that Riley's should remedy. To investigate the chain's problems in greater depth, Doug and Chris recommended that the company conduct more quantitative marketing research through a customer survey.

The First Television Advertising: The Strategy Is a Dog!

Before the quantitative research could be conducted, however, Chris and his team needed to run a new series of ads that would begin changing Riley's image. Based on past experience, Chris and his team chose television because they thought it was better for creating images. Other media are used for other purposes – radio for reinforcing images and newspaper for providing price, sales and retail store location information. At his team's urging, Chris began a campaign to sell Dave and Sam on the value of quality – meaning more expensive – television advertising.

"That was a hard sell," Chris commented as he reflected on those sessions. "They were losing money and it was really difficult to convince them to spend more to produce more polished advertising spots. They had never spent more than a few thousand dollars on a TV commercial and we wanted to spend $35,000. Also, bear in mind that we were cutting costs to the bone at $35,000."

Besides the issue of more television advertising, Chris and his team had to develop a creative strategy for the television ads. After re-reading and discussing the focus group reports numerous times, the team finally zeroed in on the theme of trust. Their research indicated that consumers were distrustful of exaggerated claims, bait 'n' switch and trade-up tactics. Obviously, consumers would like a store where they could trust the sales person and the store's level of after-sale service.

But how could they create trust through advertising? "We knew that simply saying 'Hey consumer, you can trust Riley's' wouldn't work," explained Chris. "All consumers have heard that before. We had to find some symbol of trust that everyone understands and can relate to. Finally, we hit upon the idea of a dog – after all, they're man's best friend. People are familiar with seeing-eye dogs and watch dogs. They understand that dogs can be trained to help us. So, we reasoned 'why not a consumer watchdog?' It plays off the watchdog concept that we are all familiar with so it involves no real effort for consumers to understand. In addition, the dog is a fun concept signifying that Riley's is trustworthy – approved by the watchdog. Besides, the dog could be used in other promotions...we took the dog to local baseball games, store openings and put paw prints on newspaper ads to tie our different ads together. We had a really great billboard that was actually in a Circuit City parking lot. It read 'We lift our leg on the competition' – you better believe that got attention and made the Circuit City people mad."

"We had a lot of fun with that dog, but there was one **big** problem with the dog. Because we wanted a really lovable dog, we used a golden retriever. They're one of America's favorite dogs, you know. But the only well trained dog that we could get was a female. So, Ed (the advertising name of the watch dog) was really an "Edith" – a secret that we had to guard closely."

The Quantitative Marketing Research: Listening to the Market

Even as Chris and his team were producing the Watchdog ads, Doug Barton was hard at work using the focus group results to put together a marketing research survey. The finished questionnaire was six pages long and asked for the following information:

- demographic profiles of electronic product stores
- advertising awareness levels for these
- sources of advertising used by consumers
- reasons for purchasing products
- shopping behaviors for electronic products across stores
- consumer awareness of and purchase interest in the "Home Theater" concept
- demographic questions about gender, education, income and race or ethnic group membership.

Respondents were screened on the basis of age and purchase of an electronic product in the past twelve months. In all, 343 consumers completed the questionnaire. Of these, 173 had purchased at Bud Riley's/Riley's, 100 at Circuit City and 211 at other stores.

The MARC Group, Marketing Areas Research and Consulting, Inc. of Dallas, Texas, handled the data collection. Doug used MARC because he had worked with them on research for R. J. Reynolds. As a matter of fact, MARC had done so much research for Reynolds that they had opened an office close to the Trone headquarters. This proximity sped up communication and data collection.

MARC is known for conducting telephone surveys. Their trained interviewers use computer-aided dialing and data collection techniques to generate telephone numbers, to dial and to direct the call to an interviewer when the telephone is answered. The interviewer actually records the data in the computer as the respondent answers questions. Thus, analysis can take place at any point in the data collection period to produce preliminary results.

After the data had been collected and analyzed, Doug Barton, Chris and the advertising team had just spent hours discussing the results shown in Exhibits 2 - 7.

Chris thought about all of this as he walked into the store. "Maybe actually observing some customers will give me some new ideas," he thought.

Meeting to Discuss the Campaign Theme: Prices, Sales People, Warm and Friendly?

The next day, Chris and his team were closeted in the conference room to decide on a new campaign theme. They had thoroughly reviewed the data and were quickly discovering that they did not agree on an advertising strategy – again!

"Well Chris, I said it yesterday and I'll say it again today. It's obvious what electronics customers want – low prices, wide selection and knowledgeable, caring sales staff and, in our research, Circuit City's sales staff is too pushy. People don't like that. That's where Riley's has an advantage. Leverage off that. In your television advertising – convince people that Riley's has a high quality, well trained staff that is courteous, willing to listen to them (the customer) and that they'll get great service at Kelly's," commented one of the researchers.

"Yeah," exclaimed another of the researchers. "You could show *real* sales people in the ads like Wal-Mart does. Maybe we could create a tagline about Riley's – the caring store, or the best place to shop. Give customers that real homey feeling. This is a store where they are greeted promptly and treated royally. By showing that kind of attitude, it's a cinch to convince people that they'll get good after sales service."

"I don't agree" one of the copywriters piped in. "From looking at Exhibit 7, it looks to me like Circuit City's got the selection and Riley's has the sales/service depth *and* convenient locations. We could accent good location – where you can easily find us – *and* friendly staff. How about 'the good folks *nearby*?'"

"Wait a minute," interjected the first researcher. "What people want is low prices and wide selection – the survey shows that! If we don't mention that, we aren't even in the ballpark. We have to talk about that. The data shows that while people like friendly, non-pushy sales people, they don't buy on that basis. When all is said and done, they buy the brand they want at a low price."

Another copywriter disagreed. "If we continue to beat the price and selection drum, how credible are we? We don't have a selection as great as Circuit City's and our prices are not as low as theirs – except on sale. Besides when we mention price and selection, aren't we playing to Circuit City's strength?"

"Guys, let's cool down a bit," Chris commented. "You are all making good points, but yesterday I spent time thinking about what we've done with this account. We started talking about price and product in our newspaper ads, but when we got to television, we developed a theme of trust. We got away from product-based positioning. Then, I went to a couple of stores and watched consumers. That was really, really interesting."

"This couple came in and the husband was all wound up about buying a DVD, but you could tell that the wife wasn't interested. When her husband started talking to a sales man and they were trying out new DVDs, you could see her attention wander and she looked miserable. Remember those first focus groups where we found out that men like shopping for electronics, but women don't. I wonder if we could use that as a new theme. We could try to convince consumers that shopping for electronics and appliances is fun – that it's not a chore. It would make it easier for men to get their wives and girlfriends in the stores *and* it would be in line with building an image that isn't based on product – sort of a next phase in image positioning. Maybe as long as we beat the product, price, selection drum, we aren't really differentiating ourselves from the competition. Maybe we should …"

Before Chris could finish, the researchers looked at him very skeptically. One said "Uh Chris, what are you going to tell them? That this is a party? Stick to low prices and friendly sales people. You gotta' meet the competition on the price issue and beat them with the sales people issue. Circuit City's pushing wide selection and low prices. Sears is pushing discounts and membership stores are beating the low price drum. We've got to be in the ballpark that's defined by the competition. Put low prices and good sales staff together and you've got a winning combination."

"Well, maybe…," Chris mused as he picked up the creative strategy form used by Trone. (See Exhibit 8) "So far, we have decided on the support elements and the media to use. As far as positioning is concerned, maybe it's personality that we need to be building for Riley's. And if so, what should the personality of the store be – warm, caring, convenient, attractive, fun to shop? It has to build on the recent actions taken by Dave and Sam. They've streamlined the company name, modernized and renovated stores to make them more attractive, and asked sales people to dress casually (polo shirts and slacks) rather than wearing suits and ties – just to physically differentiate themselves from the sales folks at Circuit City in the bad suits and ties. How do these actions change customer perceptions of the store? How can advertising reinforce those changes and communicate a whole new personality for the stores? Let's begin the positioning statement with:

'Riley's is the source to be trusted for home entertainment and appliances that offers … no, wait a minute… let's strike the word trust to become Riley's is the source for … When we do that, we're going to have to change some of these other elements like Consumer Proposition…"

How can Chris and his team finish the positioning statement and elements of the Creative Focus in order to attract both Dana and her husband to the store? How could they implement that positioning? Will changing advertising be sufficient or will they have to change other aspects of the store?

Other Questions for Discussion:

1. Explain how changing the newspaper ads began to change consumers' perceptions of Riley's.
2. Explain how the Watchdog campaign further changed consumers' perceptions of Riley's.
3. How is Trone using source credibility and attractiveness to change attitudes toward Riley's.
4. Describe the information search process used by electronics shoppers as shown in the Riley's research.
5. Contrast the purchase situation in a Riley's store before Dave and Sam and after Dave and Sam. How could that affect consumer purchase probability?
6. Is the sales person a social influence on the shopper? If so, how?
7. Help Chris out. What should the new re-positioning for Riley's be? Complete the creative strategy document. How would you change advertising to express the new creative strategy?

Exhibit 1
Summary of Focus Group Findings

Excerpts from focus group report:

...People shop around for electronics products. They frequently begin with Circuit City because of its extensive selection – an attribute that appeals to men. *Where* people buy is often chance – it's wherever they are when they think they have enough information to make a purchase. They buy *if* the product they have decided on is available *on the spot*, at the right price.

Consumers believe that prices do not vary from store to store and they are not attracted to promises such as a 120% price refund based on lower prices elsewhere. They think such promises as puffery. They have negative attitudes toward bait 'n' switch and they do not like to be traded up.

They begin their shopping with the Sunday paper to find out what products are available at what prices. Sales events will attract customers to stores. Once the consumer is in the store the sales person's demeanor, approach to and treatment of the customer is critical. Customers want caring, knowledgeable and organized sales people. They dislike superficial friendliness, pushiness and efforts of sales people to trade them up or sell them service contracts. The sales person should be highly knowledgeable, listen to the consumer and follow up with the customer after the sale is made.

Stores should have a wide selection, but not one that is overwhelming. Displays should be attractive and grouped by category in order to facilitate comparison shopping. Displays by brand would help consumers evaluate how all components of a system would appear in one's home – this was especially important to women as they are less concerned with price and more concerned with how the products will look in the home, i.e. whether they will blend with their decor. Men are more concerned with price, the brand name and the quality of the sound. Men enjoy shopping for electronics much more than women do and frequently, husbands narrow their product selections to a few before taking the wife in the store to look at the products.

Although men tend to be more knowledgeable about and interested in home theater, other respondents confused it with stereo television. Analysis of the research results indicates that home theatre may be in most homes in the next 5-10 years and that respondents are willing to pay about $3,000 for a system, exclusive of the television. To exploit the opportunity to sell these systems, it will be necessary to have good, long term relationships between sales people and customers as most customers will have to buy components over several purchases. To demonstrate home theatre, there should be a separate, in-store viewing area in order to give customers the "feel" of home theatre...

Exhibit 2
Demographic Profile of Shoppers

Demographic	Total %	Purchased in the last 12 months — Riley's	Circuit City	Sears	Shopped Not Purchased at Riley's	Not Shopped Not Purchased Riley's
Sex						
Male	56	56	59	60	72	43
Female	44	41	40	28	47	47
Age						
21-34	33	41	38	26	37	21
35-54	49	43	55	59	50	56
55+	18	16	7	15	13	23
Education						
High School or less	45	45	33	30	39	47
Some College	21	20	24	24	24	21
Graduated College or more	34	35	42	46	37	32
Income						
Less than $30,000	30	26	24	21	25	39
$31,000 to $49,000	36	40	34	35	36	30
$50,000 +	34	34	42	44	39	31

Exhibit 3
Advertising Awareness and Sources of Advertising Used

Type of Respondent	Top of Mind Awareness[1]	Total Unaided[2]	Total Store Awareness	Ad Awareness
Riley's Customers **Purchased from:**				
Riley's	34[3]	87	99	64
Circuit City	74	98	100	89
Sears	61	85	NA	NA
Total Shoppers **Purchased from:**				
Riley's	21	67	99	59
Circuit City	35	73	100	81
Sears	26	61	NA	NA
Source of Advertising Awareness	Riley's	Circuit City		
Radio	39	25		
Television	61	79		
Newspaper	68	72		
Mail	3	4		
Other	5	4		

[1] Top of Mind = First Store mentioned by respondent
[2] Unaided = Researcher provided no clues to help respondent answer
[3] Percentages

Exhibit 4
Shopping Behavior

Number of Stores		Purchase in Past 12 Months						
	TV	VCR	CAM	Stereo	Car Stereo	PC	Appliance	Phone
One	45	39	44	22	27	56	31	41
Two	42	40	31	56	51	22	44	29
Three	9	16	25	16	16	19	18	24
Four	4	4	--	6	3	4	5	6

Purchase of Selected Products at Riley's in Past 12 Months

Number of Stores	TV	VCR	CAM	Stereo	Car Stereo	PC	Appliance	Phone
One	56	41	NA	22	27	NA	17	NA
Two	33	27	NA	56	46	NA	51	NA
Three	8	27	NA	11	18	NA	26	NA
Four	2	--	NA	11	9	NA	6	NA

Purchase of Selected Products at Circuit City in Past 12 Months

Number of Stores	TV	VCR	CAM	Stereo	Car Stereo	PC	Appliance	Phone
One	26	25	NA	25	NA	NA	39	NA
Two	57	50	NA	63	NA	NA	54	NA
Three	3	19	NA	13	NA	NA	8	NA
Four	4	6	NA	--	NA	NA	--	NA

Shopping Behavior Between Riley's and Circuit City in Percentages

	Purchased at Riley's	Purchased at Circuit City	Purchased at Sears
Shopped Bud Riley's	100	57	16
Shopped Circuit City	73	100	

Exhibit 4 Continued

Total Items Purchased in Past 12 Months

	Riley's	Circuit City	Sears	Other
TV	28	22	13	14
VCR	15	19	10	16
CAM	9	3	5	6
Stereo	12	25	4	9
Car Stereo	6	11	5	9
PC	1	1	8	15
Appliance	26	11	52	18
Phone	3	8	4	13

Exhibit 5
Main Reasons for Purchase

Main Reasons for Purchase

	TV	VCR	CAM	Stereo	Car Stereo	PC	Appliance	Phone
Price	68	57	65	61	57	46	49	43
Service	2	3	--	1	2	10	5	3
Return	1	3	--	1	4	-	6	2
Sales	2	2	--	1	2	6	4	5
Selection	14	15	15	22	18	21	17	14
Store	3	9	8	4	5	6	9	7
Misc/Other	11	11	10	9	13	8	9	24

Total Reasons for Purchase

	TV	VCR	CAM	Stereo	Car Stereo	PC	Appliance	Phone
Price	80	74	68	80	64	60	69	53
Service	10	6	5	11	4	21	14	5
Return	8	8	5	8	13	2	12	7
Sales	8	9	8	12	7	17	14	16
Selection	32	33	25	40	34	38	28	24
Store	7	17	15	13	9	8	14	16
Misc/Other	21	14	18	19	30	19	24	36

Main Reasons for Purchase by Store

	Riley's	Circuit City	Sears	Other
Price	73	80	73	77
Selection	27	34	39	31
Service	6	7	9	6
Sales Staff	4	6	9	3
Store	8	9	12	17
Return Policy	4	6	17	5
Miscellaneous	17	21	24	25

15

Exhibit 6
Mean Store Ratings by Place of Purchase

		Mean Store Ratings		
Attribute	Riley's	Circuit City	Sears	Shopped/Not Purchased BR
Overall shopping satisfaction	5.25	5.29	5.33	4.49
Low prices	4.85	5.20	4.11	4.04
Wide product selection	5.28	5.69	5.24	4.85
Wide brand selection	5.12	5.70	5.07	4.91
Quality merchandise	5.47	5.66	5.38	5.31
Good/convenient location	5.49	5.12	5.28	5.39
Trustworthy/caring sales staff	4.90	4.68	4.60	4.51
Advertised merchandise available	5.28	5.28	5.16	5.08
Non-pushy/aggressive sales staff	5.05	4.85	4.93	4.57
Knowledgeable sales staff	5.21	5.16	4.85	4.47
Hassle free return policy	5.02	5.47	5.51	4.90
Provides quality service	5.05	5.22	5.44	4.32
Has attractive financing offers	5.30	5.00	5.03	4.55
Quick delivery	5.13	5.31	5.08	4.92
Sales staff greeted in timely manner	5.26	4.96	4.86	4.64

16

Exhibit 7
Cross-Store Comparisons

	Riley's	Circuit City	Sears
Convenience	.80[1]	-.20	0.00
Sales and Service Department	.20	-.20	.01
Low Prices	.10	.38	-.50
Scope of Selection	-.18	.48	-.30

[1] Scale runs from –1.0 to 1.0; data is relative rather than absolute

Exhibit 8
CREATIVE STRATEGY

<u>Brand/Store Overview</u>

Positioning Statement   Riley's is the source for …

Marketing Objective   Re-position chain to…

Competition   Circuit City and Sears

<u>Creative Focus</u>

Current Belief   Price is the most important reason for purchase followed by selection and service.

Consumer Proposition   As a major player in the electronics and appliance business, Riley's offers a true value for the consumer dollar. Value is measured in terms of better prices, good selection and considerate service before and after the sale. As a competitive edge, Riley's …

Support Elements[1]   Riley's carries top name brand merchandise at better prices, offers special financing and provides superior service after the sale through the largest service center in North Carolina. Consumer trust is built by Riley's generous exchange and refund policies.

Desired Belief   Riley's is…

Store Personality

Executional Considerations

Primary: print with emphasis on multi-page inserts. TV.
Secondary: Radio, direct mail.

[1] These are facts that about the store that can be used to support the advertised image.

Burlington and the UPF Clothing Market

When Alan S. was leafing through the latest LL Bean catalog looking for clothes to wear on a skiing trip, he noticed a little sun pictured below a shirt. Wondering what the sun meant, he flipped back to the symbols description to find that the sun stood for UPF protection greater than 15 for the garment. Thoughts of UPF protection led to thoughts about glare from snow – glare that went everywhere – in one's eyes, face, hands and any other exposed part of the body. "Hm-m-m-m," he thought, "maybe I ought to get that shirt or better yet a jacket with UPF protection…"

While Alan is looking for a jacket with UPF protection, Mark Cumiskey of Burlington Industries' PerformanceWear Division, is also thinking about UPF clothing, but his thoughts are quite different. He wants to know how to convince Alan and others to buy those UPF garments because that's part of his job. He wonders what are the most likely targets for UPF clothing, how to create awareness for the product and what are the most effective ways to motivate purchase. Mark has all sorts of information at his fingertips about the increasingly deadly effects of melanoma (very serious skin cancer). Is that information, however, powerful enough to motivate purchase? After all, there is a price for UPF clothing. The fabric to make such garments does cost a little more. Will consumers *buy* increased sun protection?

Mark's problem is complicated because most consumers aren't aware of the need for sun or UPF protection in clothing. By now, most of them have heard that they should always use SPF lotions to protect their skin when in the sun, but many of them don't bother for a variety of reasons – they won't be in the sun long; they'll be in the shade; it's too much bother or they haven't gotten skin cancer yet, so why would they now? (Only two out of every five people consistently use sunscreen when exposed to the sun.) "If they won't use lotion, then how I am going to get them to use UPF clothing?" mused Mark. "How do I make them aware of the problem? How do I get them to look for UPF clothing? How can I convince them to pay more for these clothes and how do I get them to buy UPF clothing made from Burlington fabrics? And who should I be trying to convince?"

Of course, there are the Alans of the world – young outdoor enthusiasts who spend a lot of time in the sun. They are an obvious target, but they've usually spent 15 years or so in the sun already without UPF clothing. For them, much of the damage has already been done as 80% of sun exposure occurs before the age of 18. Are they going to be persuaded that they need such clothing after all these years?

Maybe there are other segments in the market that would be more receptive to this product. Parents – in particular, mothers of young children – might be a good market. They would naturally want to protect their children, and it's well known that younger skin burns more easily than older skin. Mark was heartened to read not long ago that parents of young children are spending far more than their parents did on their children. "If they'll buy those expensive umbrella strollers and Spanish lessons for little kids, why wouldn't they buy UPF clothing?" Mark wonders.

Then, there are other segments. What about gardeners – either home gardeners or professional ones? They spend considerable time in the sun, as do construction workers, policemen and golfers.

Skin Protection and Cancer

As increasing numbers of Americans spend more time in the sun, the chances of skin cancer are accelerating. In 1935, 1 in 1,500 people were projected to develop malignant skin cancer, melanoma; today that projection is 1 in 75 and 1 in 5 people will develop some form of skin cancer. Each year, dermatologists estimate that one million Americans develop skin cancer. The real damage is exposure over time. Most sun damage occurs in children under 15 years of age, but it won't turn into skin cancer until 20-30 years later when they are reaching middle age.

To make matters worse, children burn much faster than adults. One hour in the sun for an adult equals 4 minutes for a baby. In the length of time that it takes Mom to strap a child into a stroller, adjust her pocketbook and push that stroller across a parking lot to stores, a beach or a park, a baby could theoretically develop sunburn. Even if she does this in the shade, the ultraviolet rays that cause sunburn may reach the child as ultraviolet rays can reflect off snow, water and sand, and clouds do not filter out the harmful rays on overcast days.

Of course, as the child gets older, it takes longer for them to burn, but then they also are prone to spend more time outside, swimming, bike riding and engaging in other activities. They could protect themselves with lotion, but that often leaves a greasy feeling on the skin, only lasts for one and a half-hours and has to be re-applied more and more frequently as its effectiveness declines with repeated use on the same day. It's hard to imagine children transporting lotion with them and remembering to use it. After all, they do not see the damage right away and neither do their parents and carefully smearing themselves with lotion is a geeky thing to do!

How does skin cancer occur? Ultraviolet B rays, dubbed the "burning rays" target the upper layers of skin and can actually break down DNA and RNA, causing free-radical damage and cell mutation. The real culprits, however, are the ultraviolet A rays or, as they are called, "the silent killers," that penetrate the skin further and destroy the collagen matrix. This disturbance of genetic material and cell formation is one of the factors that lead to the development of skin cancer.

There are three types of skin cancer: (1) basal cell carcinomas, (2) squamous cell carcinomas and (3) malignant melanoma, which is potentially life threatening. Most skin cancers start as basal cell carcinomas and if untreated or unrecognized, can progress to melanoma. The occurrence of melanoma is increasing at a rate of 3% annually which doesn't sound too bad until one considers that melanoma is the most common form of cancer in women aged twenty to twenty-nine, the second most common form of cancer in women aged thirty to thirty-four (behind breast cancer) and is the fifth most common form of cancer overall in the United States behind lung, breast, colon and prostrate cancers. Melanoma shows up as pigmented spots that are irregular in any way (shape, size, color, and symmetry) or are growing. Depending on their bodily location (on the back), they may not be discovered early on for treatment. Furthermore, as table 1 indicates, some skin types are more likely to burn than others are.

Table 1 Sensitivity of Skin Types to Sunburn

Type Skin	Type Sensitivity	Characteristics
I	Extremely	Always burns, never tans--Celtic
II	Very	Burns easily, tans minimally
III	Average	Burns moderately – Caucasians
IV	Minimally	Always tans well to moderately brown – olive skin
V	Rarely	Tans well to a dark brown – brown skin
VI	Never	Deeply pigmented – black skin

Source: Tondl, 1999

As the threat from melanoma increases, consumers can react in several ways. The most obvious is to stay out of the sun, but that is contradictory to the increasingly active lifestyles of many young Americans, which is encouraged by physicians. Thirty minutes of exercise each day is after all good for one's heart and our leaders such as presidents Clinton and Bush set an example by jogging. Millions more Americans are skiing, hiking, snow boarding, skating and wind surfing. A second way to reduce skin cancer is using lotions, but as we've already seen, many Americans although well aware that they should use SPF lotions fail to do so.

A third means of protecting skin is to wear UPF clothing but at present there are few such garments offered and most are not widely available in retail stores. Usually UPF clothing is available only through catalogers who expend limited effort in promoting these garments. The companies that sell UPF rated garments include LL Bean, Liz Claiborne, Orvis, Sportif, the Wise Child, Sun Precautions, Sun Wise, Great Provision Outdoor Company, The North Face and Patagonia among others. Thus, coupled with lack of awareness on the part of consumers is lack of availability and lack of promotion.

UPF Clothing

Ultraviolet Protection Factor, UPF, is a textile classification that determines a fabric's rate of protection from harmful ultraviolet A and ultraviolet B radiation. SPF or Sun Protection Factor is the acronym assigned to sunscreen lotions and cosmetics. Why two types of protection factors? UPF is tested in vitro which means through instrumental measurements. SPF is tested in vivo, on the human body. One can interpret both ratings in a similar fashion. If one is wearing a UPF garment or SPF lotion with a rating of 15, that individual could stay in the sun for 150 minutes before being burnt. UV protection and UPF protection are related, but not the same. Any garment claiming UV% of 50% is actually equivalent to an UPF rating of 2 which means one would burn in one-half the time versus no protection at all. (See Table 2.) Obviously it takes a lot of UV% filtration to produce an acceptable UPF rating!

Table 2 Relationship of UV protection and UPF protection

UV%	UPF
50%	2
75	4
90	10
93	15
95	20
97	33
98	50
99	100
99.9	1,000

Source: Outfitter Magazine (1999, July), p. 39

There are several ways to increase the UPF of a garment. First, fiber producers such as DuPont, Nylstar and Sterling Fibers offer acrylic, polyester and/or nylon fibers with an additive that improves the UPF rating. These fibers are made into yarns, then fabrics and finally into finished garments. Second, textile producers can construct fabrics with many ends and picks per inch. By doing so, the construction of the fabric mechanically blocks the harmful UVR. Companies such as Burlington Industries, Milliken & Co., AlliedSignal and DuPont use this approach. Also, Ciba Specialty Chemical offers a chemical treatment that can be applied to fabric to increase UPF. Third, garments can be constructed to reduce exposure to the sun. For example, longer sleeves and hats with longer bills or flaps that cover the back of the neck would reduce exposure. Given style constraints (who wants to wear a hat with a flap in the back?) the easiest means of increasing UPF protection through clothing is to buy UPF rated garments.

Burlington and UPF Clothing

Burlington's Industries is one of the largest softgoods manufacturers in the world; employs approximately 19,000 people; has plants in three states, Mexico, and India, and has been committed since its founding to the development and production of innovative fabrics. Demonstrating market savvy and progressive ideas, it was one of the first firms to produce rayon in 1924. Within a few years it became the nation's leading producer of rayon – even though the firm itself was less than ten years old. Since then, the company has grown through a combination of acquisitions, global expansion and introduction of new products. (For more information on Burlington, go to www.Burlington.com.)

Of its five divisions, Burlington PerformanceWear is one of the most exciting as it combines luxury, technology, fashion, function, style and value in its fabrics and garments. This division makes a wide range of products from women's wear, men's slacks, blazers and suits, high-tech activewear, uniforms and protective products for medical and clean room uses.

Burlington produces a variety of performance fabrics, fibers and systems. Some of these are: (1) Xalt – a high-tech composite system that combines fabric and laminate technology for superior waterproof, breathable, windproof comfort and protection. During workouts, Xalt breathes away perspiration to keep the wearer dry and comfortable. (2) Versatech is a combination of a specially designed, superfine, tightly woven microfiber yarn and a water repellent finish that makes it resistant to water penetration. (3) Durepel is a water and stain repellent finish designed to keep wearers drier longer. (4) Micromove is a lightweight, breathable, soft and drapable microfiber fabric designed to be lightweight and move with the body. (5) 3D Dimension is a unique, woven fleece, that provides more stretch, is water repellent, and is waterproof and windproof. (6) Moisture Control System (M.C.S.) is outdoor sportswear fabric for high aerobic activity that absorbs, wicks and dries faster than cotton.

UPF clothing is found in the M.C.S. Blocker system. M.C.S. is a specifically designed synthetic fabric, either nylon or polyester, that works well for strenuous, high-aerobic activities. On this fabric, the M.C.S. is dispersed over a wider surface than conventional fabrics with the result that the fabric dries more quickly than cotton does. It also doesn't stick to the wearer. The addition of the term, Blocker, to M.C.S. adds another feature to the fabric which is protection from the sun. The phrase UPF30 is contained within the O of the subbrand Blocker to attract the consumer's attention and quickly communicate this benefit. Communication of M.C.S. benefits to the consumer is through a hangtag that can be affixed to the finished garment.

The front of the hangtag contains the name of the brand, M.C. S. BLOCKER, with "moisture control system" spelled out in smaller letters and the company and division product names, Burlington and PerformanceWear fabrics, at the bottom. Inside on the left half of the tag, the main benefits of the product are highlighted as "More advanced…" "More protection…" "More strength…", "More comfort…" The UPF feature is mentioned under the more protection section as a UPF rating of 30, even when wet. This feature is prominently emphasized on the right half of the tag with the headline "M.C. S. Blocker maintains its UPF 30 rating…" The bullet points under this headline indicate that launderings, abrasion, continuous exposure to light, perspiration, and exposure to chlorinated pool water will not damage the SPF rating. The hangtag is a combination of oranges, yellows and bright pinks, which makes it highly noticeable. At present, the hangtag is Mark's main form of communication to consumers.

Because Burlington does not sell these PerformanceWear products directly to consumers, it must work with its customers, which are companies such as LL Bean, to promote the specific fabrics, fibers and treatments. When a cataloger places an order, Burlington sends the fabric to the catalogers' cutter to begin the manufacture of a garment, which will be finished in a plant that supplies the cataloger. As a result, a shirt made of M.C.S. Blocker fabric may have the LL Bean or Patagonia brand name on the inside label. Specifics of the garments' construction and materials are appended as hangtags by the company packaging the garments for the cataloger. Thus, consumers may never see Mark's hangtags unless LL Bean and other customers are willing to affix them to garments made from M.C.S. Blocker.

Through cooperative advertising, Burlington can get additional promotional push for their fabrics through mentions in the catalog and designations such as the sun that Alan saw.

Through this co-branding effort, the names of Burlington and companies such as LL Bean, Land's End and Patagonia can reinforce each other's quality image.

The problem with this arrangement is that other textile firms, Milliken & Co., AlliedSignal and DuPont, can supply UPF rated fabrics and all of these manufacturers would like to have hangtags denoting their UPF fabrics on finished garments. From the cataloger's point of view, this becomes a problem as the garments made from one textile producer's fabric must be carefully distinguished from another in order to match the right hangtag with a garment made from the right fabric. Given that the fabrics from multiple manufacturers may feed into the same cut and sew operations making a variety of garments for the cataloger, this tracking of fabrics in order to apply the appropriate hangtags can be a real nuisance. In addition, one has to wonder how many final consumers actually read all the hangtags affixed to any garment rather than just cutting off the hangtags and throwing them away? Is their confidence in the brand primarily placed in the catalogers' brand or in the brands of suppliers to the cataloger?

Mark has a dream of rivaling "Gore-Tex" in the breathable, waterproof fabric world. The Gore-Tex brand, which is widely known and has generated high brand preference and loyalty, is actually a textile manufacturer's brand. It is made by W. L. Gore, a specialist firm in flouropolymer technology and manufacturing. Fabrics are only one of its divisions – others include electronics, filtration and separation devices, medial and health care products, and sealants. Gore-Tex is, however, one of the company's best known brands and one can find firemen, military personnel, doctors and health care professionals, police and outdoor enthusiasts wearing garments and uniforms that are breathable, windproof and waterproof – thanks to Gore.

To achieve high brand recognition, W. L. Gore uses consumer advertising which costs them over $1.2 million annually, has an active web site (www.goretex.com) which promotes Gore-Tex and sends web users to the retailers that sell garments made of Gore-tex, and insists that all garments made of Gore-Tex not only have hangtags, but also have a Gore-Tex label sewn into an inside or outside seam on all products. In newer products, the brand name may be embroidered on the sleeve or chest of the garment or be found on a small metal tag on the outside. To maintain quality control, only a limited number of specialist garment manufacturers are licensed to use the fabric. To ensure water tightness, Gore produces Gore-Seam Tape that can be used to close any holes created while sewing seams. To help consumers select the garment that is right for them and the intended use, Gore-Tex produces a number of hangtags such as an EXTREME WET WEATHER tag. A quick check of the LL Bean catalog indicates that Gore sells garments that are co-branded, LLBean's Gore-Tex Microsuede Rain Parka and items under the Gore-Tex brand only – Gore-Tex Mountain Guide Parka.

To rival Gore-Tex, Burlington would have to stimulate secondary demand through a pull strategy aimed at final consumers. This would require generating demand for individual brands such as M.C.S. Blocker by spending millions of dollars on consumer advertising. At present, many of Burlington's advertising dollars are aimed at corporate advertising promoting the Burlington name. It should be noted that Burlington was the first textile company to engage in network television advertising way back in 1955, so advertising *does* have a long tradition at Burlington.

Burlington has manufacturing plants that could make apparel under a Burlington brand name, but then those garments would compete with the current items at LL Bean and other apparel firms that use the M.C.S. Blocker brand. LLBean would then view Burlington as a competitor and might move away from co-branding garments with Burlington with the result that Burlington would lose the quality reinforcement gained through co-branding with LLBean.

At present, Mark needs to decide whether UPF rating is a feature that would compel consumer purchase if Burlington did beef up its advertising. Actually, Mark and Burlington are ahead of some other manufacturers by producing UPF-rated fabric. In countries such as Australia and New Zealand, classifications for sun protective clothing have been in use since 1996. In the U.S., a sub-committee of the American Society for Testing and Materials (ASTM) which is regulated by the Consumer Products Safety Commission and the Federal Trade Commission is charged with setting standards and measurements for UV-protective clothing. Once those standards are set, all clothing could be UPF rated and firms might be required to indicate those ratings on labels. If that happens, Burlington could have a significant lead in the marketplace if it advertises its UPF textiles or garments now. The problem is whether consumers will actually use UPF ratings to make purchase decisions.

In addition, Mark has to decide what market segments to target – gardeners, parents of small children, construction, and other outdoor workers. He also has to determine the best means to reach the market. Is it hangtags with or without co-operative advertising? Are the hangtags that he has now sufficient to "sell" consumers on M.C.S. Blocker?

From a more long run perspective, should he and Burlington even consider competing directly with Gore by making M.C.S. Blocker garments? Is there room in the market for two breathable, waterproof, windproof brands of outer wear?

Questions for Discussion:

1. The case identifies three general targets for UPF clothing: parents of young children, young outdoor enthusiasts and individuals who work outdoors (gardeners and construction workers). What kind of motives would each of these groups have in regard to purchasing UPF clothing? Would these be approach or avoidance?
2. What kind of learning would each group need to engage in to be convinced to buy this kind of clothing?
3. How would lifestyle affect the need for UPF clothing?
4. What kind of appeals might be effective in convincing these consumers to buy UPF clothing?
5. How could the self-concept be used to explain purchase of UPF clothing?

References:

-----, "Sun protective fabrics turning on the heat," Sporting Goods Business, 1998, July, p. 34.

-----, "Sunscreen should include UV-A protection," USA Today, 1999, July, pp. 6-7.

-----, "T-shirts inadequate against sun's rays," Dermatology Times, 1995, April, p. 66.

Sun Protective Clothing – Evaluation and Classification, 1996, Australian/New Zealand Standards, p. 4

Autier, P., Dore, J., Negrier, S. Leinard, D. , "Sunscreen Use and Duration of Sun Exposure: A double-blind, randomized trial," <u>Journal of the National Cancer Institute</u>, 1999, August, pp. 1302-1309.

Davis, S., "Relationship of fiber type, mass and coer to the sun protection factor of fabrics," University of Alberta, 1995.

Emmons, K., and Colditz, G. "Preventing Excess Sun Exposure: It is time for a national policy," <u>Journal of the National Cancer Ins</u>titute, 1999, August, pp. 1269-1270.

Maier, K. "Hot Summer Skin Protection," <u>Better Nutrition</u>, 1999, June, pp. 66-88.

Pate, R.R. and Pratt, M. "Physical activity and public health: A recommendation from the Centers of Disease Control and Prevention and the American College of Sports Medicine, <u>JAMA</u>, 1995, v. 273 n. 5, pp. 402-7.

Schwartz, R. FDA Torches Sunscreen SPFs Greater Than 30," <u>American Druggist</u>, 1999, July, p. 22.

Simonson, S. Telephone Interview, Burlington Industries, 1999, October, Hurt, VA.

Stone, J. "Hats for Sun Protection," <u>Journal of Family and Consumer Sciences</u>, 1999, June, pp. 146-9.

Straley, C. "Outsmarting the Sun: Play it safe with our skin-saving strategies," <u>Parents Magazine</u>, 1995, June, pp. 146-9.

Textile Institute, The, "Apparel Textiles and Sun Protection, <u>Niches in the World of Textiles</u>, 1996, May, pp. 180-189.

Tondl, R. "Sun's Up! Cover Up!" <u>Journal of Family and Consumer Sciences</u>, 1999, v. 66, p. 92.

Tye, L. "Rising skin cancer rates 'frightening'," <u>The San Diego Union-Tribune</u>, 1997, April 6, p. D12.

When Heroes Leave Us:
The Case of Dale Earnhardt

About 12 years ago, a colleague at work gave Larry R. tickets to a NASCAR Winston Cup Race. Although Larry knew nothing about NASCAR, he went anyway. Big mistake – he was hooked. Over the next decade, he and his family attended at least 2 Winston Cup races a year and watched all the others on television. In particular, he became a fan of Dale Earnhardt, infamous #3, in the Goodwrench car.

Like most fans, Larry started by buying a t-shirt with his hero on it, and then a model car and then a box of Wheaties, etc. The hobby just grew and grew. There were Dale Earnhardt cars, belt buckles, ceiling fan, sheets, sunglasses, books, souvenirs of various races, socks and other clothing, patches from races and much more. Where did Larry put all of this stuff? In his and his wife's bedroom. They slept on those Earnhardt sheets, under the Earnhardt fan and looked at Earnhardt memorabilia last thing at night and first thing in the morning.

Did this bother Karen, the wife? Not really. She viewed it as a harmless hobby; she thought that Larry worked hard and this was his only interest. Furthermore, it kept him at home and she and the children actually enjoyed going to the races. In the summer, they went to races in Daytona, visited her parents in Orlando and went to the beach, Disney World, and Epcot Center. The Winston Cup circuit had become part of their summer vacation. They found the race crowd to be mostly well behaved and it made for a good family outing. They even joined the prestigious E Club for serious Earnhardt fans. Through that membership, they were able to get more information about NASCAR, races and of course Dale and his exploits, as well as attend private parties for E Club members. In addition, Larry collected everything he could read about Dale Earnhardt.

Eventually, the Earnhardt collection outgrew their bedroom. Although Larry had had cabinets built to display his collection and to maximize the opportunity to display Earnhardt souvenirs, the collection was just too big for the bedroom. What do you think Larry did?

He built a bigger house with five bedrooms, one for he and his wife, one for each child and the other two, he knocked into one room to display the Earnhardt collection. Now, there were life-sized cutouts of Earnhardt, coolers, grills, furniture, and Kleenex. When they moved into the new house, Karen had a couple of Earnhardt cars soldered to the ends of drapery rods as finials to set off the black drapes. You name it; Larry had it.

In 1999, he made a wonderful discovery – Ebay – where he could buy and sell Earnhardt memorabilia to his heart's content. Wife Karen kept track of whether the expenditures exceeded the inflow. Like most serious NASCAR fans, Larry had learned to order model cars before they reached market and he frequently bought more than one item. Buying, selling and trading was a major part of the game for him. Besides the hours he spent on the computer with the Earnhardt goods, he and Karen visited NASCAR dealers in several states and left their card. Sellers frequently called them with unique Earnhardt articles. By the beginning of 2000, the value of Larry's collection easily exceeded $30,000 by Larry's estimates which is a lot of boxes of Wheaties!

Then, it all ended suddenly. On Sunday, February 18, 2001, Earnhardt collided with Sterling Martin and was knocked by another car into the wall. Earnhardt died instantly. At the time of Earnhardt's death, Larry had been working on a train that would run around the Earnhardt room and go through the wall into the closet and come out on the other side. After the race that Sunday, he had planned to finish the openings in the walls. Five days later, he hadn't even been in the Earnhardt room. Why? "All the fun is gone," he said. According to Karen, Larry had always said he would sell the Earnhardt collection when Dale quit racing, but Larry never thought it would end like this and he couldn't face the collection. He was in shock.

Millions of fans collected at memorial services, at the church where the funeral was held and at races to mourn the loss of Dale Earnhardt. The media made the most of it covering the thousand-mile pilgrimages of fans, airing the tearful interviews with fans of all ages, and broadcasting a memorial service across the U.S. In addition, there was a flood of Internet, magazine, newspaper, radio and television tributes. One Georgian wrote in the Atlanta-Constitution, "Stock car racing's greatest now runs with God and a host of departed drivers on a speedway in heaven and in all likelihood, he is bumping God going around."

Unlike Larry, many fans wanted Earnhardt merchandise, which flew off shelves. They lined up at shops like Pro Image and NASCAR Thunder and all Earnhardt merchandise was gone within two hours. Prices for Earnhardt goods on Ebay shot up. In less than a month, autographed pictures had gone from $15 to nearly $760; die-cast cars soared from $60 to over $300. Worse yet, thieves from Ohio to South Carolina were stealing Coke vending machines bearing a life-size image of Earnhardt and moving them on flatbed trucks. One was offered on Ebay for $12,000, but no one bought it. Three photofronts of Earnhardt pried off the machines did sell for $450. When Larry re-financed his house, the bank had the Dale Earnhardt collection appraised. The value in April 2001? Over $200,000.

Why all of this outpouring of grief for a stock car driver? For a man who spent most of his career seeing fans waving signs that said "Anyone but Earnhardt"? According to one writer, Dale was Elvis Presley on wheels. He spoke to something in working class America and never seemed to forget where he came from. One of four children with a race-car-driving father who was barely able to make ends meet, Dale quit school after the eighth grade, took his first driving job for grocery money. He never seemed to change. Even as a celebrity worth millions, he still shopped at Wal-Mart and stood in line.

After coming in 22nd in his first Winston Cup race in 1975, he never looked back, winning 76 Winston Cup races in the next 20 years. He was trying to make sure that his racing team would finish one-two when he collided with Sterling Marlin with whom he was jockeying for third place.

A ferocious competitor, Earnhardt was brash, outspoken ("I want to give more than 100 percent every race, and if that's aggressive, then I reckon I am."), wild and reckless – often bumping other drivers on the track and threading between drivers where there seemed to be no room – all of which earned him the nickname, **The Intimidator**. He was the embodiment of the rural southern male of yore – independent and macho. His style recalled other reckless drivers who crashed and burned early in their careers – Fireball Roberts and Tiny Lund. These were the early rebels and cowboys who fueled the growth of NASCAR at its beginning. While NASCAR had grown up, gotten more sophisticated, gone upscale and become less rowdy, Dale Earnhardt had not. He was still bumping cars, taking licks, refusing to use modern safety equipment and crashing cars – no matter what the consequences. He was not phony; he was a winner and he epitomized values and an approach to life that many admired.

Sports psychologists tell us that people become fans of teams or individuals because they want to be part of something bigger. Maybe they want to be winners; so they become Yankees fans. Maybe they want to be part of an image –Dale's aw shucks, southern good-old boy act – or they want to bask in the reflected glory. They perceive the departure of heroes as the end of an era. When Kennedy died, Camelot ended. When Jordan left the Bulls, their domination of the NBA declined. When Martin Luther King died, the dream faltered. When Dale Earnhardt leaves NASCAR, the ties to the boisterous past are gone.

The same sports psychologists tell us that commitment (being a fan) begins with a small act and one behavior leads to another. These behaviors persist and grow because the individual enjoys them, finds that they speak to something inside of one and enables one to express or act out through our heroes attitudes and behaviors that we cannot do in our lives. Like Larry says, "Earnhardt was fun. He bumped drivers; he made them mad; you never knew what daring stunt he would pull next; it kept you watching." He successfully defied authority.

His death leaves a big void for NASCAR and fans. This was to have been the dream season of NASCAR. It had its biggest television contract ever and licensing of products had soared to new levels. As the fastest growing sport in the U.S., NASCAR was primed to become the biggest sport in the U.S. by overtaking pro-football. So, Dale Earnhardt died at possibly the worst time for NASCAR and plunged officials into a nightmare – how to show respect for Earnhardt without appearing to be exploiting his death.

What happens to revenues and popularity when *the driver, the man* that the fans come to see, dies? Dale Earnhardt and Jeff Gordon alone accounted for about 70 percent of NASCAR merchandise sales. Larry's observation that droves of fans left the stands when Earnhardt left a race, that they came to see Dale whether they loved him or hated him, underscores the importance of Earnhardt to NASCAR revenues. Some observers believe that Earnhardt fans will merely shift their loyalty to Dale Earnhardt Jr. But he isn't the same personality that his father was.

Major corporations committed to contracts with Earnhardt faced the same dilemma. Should they appear callous by going ahead with sales of Earnhardt merchandise? Coca-Cola pulled ads featuring Earnhardt. ConAGra Foods destroyed over 100,000 cans of Van Camps beans bearing Earnhardt's likeness. How do these actions affect fans? Which group of fans do these companies satisfy when they dump the Earnhardt products – the Larry's or the fans who bought the merchandise after Earnhardt's death?

And what of General Motors who had sponsored Earnhardt for years in the #3 Goodwrench car? Companies know that NASCAR fans are extremely loyal to their drivers. Studies by Performance Research show that more than 70 percent of NASCAR fans consciously choose NASCAR sponsors' products over other brands while only 30 – 50% of fans of other sports exhibit brand loyalty.

That loyalty translates into big bucks. Before DuPont sponsored Jeff Gordon, the automotive-refinishes group was a $500 million business. In 1999, their sales exceeded $1 billion dollars. Lou Savelli of DuPont attributes 20% of that growth to the association with Gordon and says he earns $5 for every $1 he spends on Gordon. Sponsors cover the $9 to $11 million it takes to put a driver on the track. Even The Intimidator commented "Without 'em (sponsors), we're a bunch of broken-down old cars." In the world of television advertising, $9 to $11 million is a drop in the bucket. It can cost several million to film a 30-second ad and much more than that to air it. But for the same dollars, advertisers get their logo on a stockcar shown over and over during the Winston Cup races for hours at a time to audiences of tens of millions of people who may be highly loyal to the brand. It would be cost prohibitive for companies to buy that much exposure in other ways. With whom can General Motors replace Dale Earnhardt? Should or how can they capitalize on their association with Earnhardt?

Different fans deal with grief in different ways. Some retreat while others rush out to buy mementos. There's money to be made in the death or departure of heroes whether politicians (Kennedy memorabilia soared in price) or athletes and some company will always be around to take advantage of that.

Discussion Questions:

1. Use the sports psychologists' explanations to explain how Larry became a Dale Earnhardt fan. Does this differ from the concept of involvement? If so, how? If not, what type of involvement is this? How might this be related to brand loyalty?

2. What type of learning did Larry engage in?

3. Obviously Larry had strong attitudes toward Dale Earnhardt? What elements comprise that attitude? What factors in his environment reinforce that attitude?

4. Why is Larry unwilling to be involved with the Earnhardt collection after Earnhardt's death? Why do other fans buy merchandise?

5. How can NASCAR deal with the loss of a revenue maker like Earnhardt? Should they issue Earnhardt memorabilia?

6. Should Coca-Cola have pulled their ads? Should ConAgra have dumped those beans?

7. What should General Motors do? Capitalize on their association with Earnhardt in some way? If so, how? Should they find another driver?

8. Will Dale Senior's fans shift their loyalty to Dale Junior? Why or why not?

9. Think of one of your heroes who has either retired or died. Compare that situation with the situation after Earnhardt's death. Are the same market and consumer forces at work?

10. What do you think Larry will do with the Earnhardt collection?

References:

-------, "Such Intimidating Prices on Ebay," <u>Business Week</u>, March 12, 2001, p. 14.

-------, "The Fastest Growing Sport Loses its Hero," <u>U.S. News & World Report</u>, March 5, 2001, v. 130, p. 52.

Banks, Margaret Moffett, "From Grief to Healing," Greensboro News & Record, February 25, 2001, p. A1:A10.

Heisler, Eric and Amy Joyner, "A Collectibles Champion," <u>Greensboro News and Record</u>, February 24, 2001, pp. B10, B13.

Hewitt, Bill, Don Sider and Michaele Ballard, "A Hero's Last Lap," <u>People Weekly</u>, March 5, 2001, pp. 100-106.

Johnson, Roy S. "Speed Sells," Fortune, April 12, 1999, pp. 56-70.

Koster, Kim, "True Blue," <u>Duke Magazine</u>, January-February 2001, pp. 2 –8,

Long, Dustin, "First-lap wreck brings back memories," Greensboro News & Record, February 26, 2001, p. C1:C5.

McGinn, Molly, "Fans search for relief at race," Greensboro News & Record, February 26, 2001, p. A1; A6.

Underwood, Stephen, "A Year like No Other for NASCAR," <u>Sporting Goods Business,</u> March 9, 2001, v. 34, p. 38ff.

CASE 4

Vampyres: Strangers in the Night?

Question: What do Bela Lugosi, Frank Langella, Tom Cruise, Brad Pitt and Willem Dafoe have in common? Answer: They've all been vampires – in the movies. Lugosi in the thirties, Langella in the eighties, Cruise and Pitt in the nineties and Dafoe in 2001, thus proving that vampires have lasting value!

We all know about vampires – they drink blood, never die, can't stand the smell of garlic, come from Transylvania, sleep in coffins, constantly prey on helpless females, are afraid of the cross, and have to be killed by driving a stake through their heart. At least, that was the common perception of vampires until the nineties. They were the undead and they were bad news.

Then the nineties saw the upmarketisation of the horror genre. Starting with *Silence of the Lambs* (1991), followed by *Bram Stoker's Dracula* (1992), *Mary Shelley's Frankenstein* (1994) and then *Interview with the Vampire* (1998), horror reached new heights of popularity. Thanks to Anne Rice, author of the popular *Vampire Chronicles*, the vampire is no longer a dreaded, feared figure. Instead the vampire is an outsider – perhaps longing to be inside. They are always seeking other vampires, meeting in secret places known only to their kind and form a sort of outsider subculture. They become sympathetic figures. Think of Louis (Brad Pitt) who is so lonely and in spiritual agony over his condition which even he despises. Furthermore, he is antagonistic to Lestat, played by Tom Cruise (now, there's a vampire that we can dislike). So, Louis became the "good" vampire (he bemoaned his nature) pitted against the evil vampire.

These are dark, brooding, even romantic figures like Heathcliff from the Brontes; Rochester in Jane Eyre; or Stanley Kowalski in *A Streetcar Named Desire*. This is the dangerous and beautiful man – a sort of deadly attraction of the unknown. As the vampires flit through life, death follows in a meaningless and random manner. Sustaining life requires the transmission of blood from victim to vampire. The blood-letting becomes an erotic ritual of its own. As the victim weakens, the vampire becomes giddy and then strong from the blood. The renewal of life that the blood brings expresses an intense lust for life – a refusal to die or forego what gives them life.

Although the vampires bring death, they anguish over the deaths of their loved ones – Louis for his brother and Lestat for his mother. Thus, they become somehow human, are able to love others and mourn death even though they are the cause of it.

This is really not a happy subject, but obviously it's a fascinating one to many people as the popularity of vampire movies and books attest. Besides Anne Rice's books, there are a number of vampire books that have appeared on the scene. Books such as *A Coven of Vampires* by Brian Lumley and *Piercing the Darkness: Undercover with Vampires in America Today* by Katherine Ramsland feed the vampire frenzy.

Vampires are also on the small screen – television. One of the most popular television series is *Buffy the Vampire Slayer* in which Buffy, played by Sarah Michelle Gellar, kills vampires, witches and even giant Preying Mantises that threaten her community. Buffy is a perky college student who has moved to Sunnyvale to attend college. Unfortunately Sunnydale is located on a "Hellmouth" – a demon filled void which spews forth underworld bad guys and gals that she must slay – all while dating normal guys and going to college.

Buffy is a production of Warner Brothers (WB), which is owned by AOL Time Warner. Although not as big a success as *ER* or *The Practice*, it has attracted a very loyal cult following, turned Ms. Gellar into a star, established WB as a legitimate player and is the basis for WB's young, hip image. Buffy has an intense Internet following – so intense that Twentieth Century Fox (which buys Buffy from WB) had to crack down on fan sites for copyright infringement. Following in Buffy's wake is *Angel* in which a dark male angel battles constantly against his nature to protect the "good" from the forces of evil.

This phenomenon is not confined to the U.S. In Southeast Asia, *My Date With a Vampire* nabbed almost all the major awards (Most Popular TV Programme, Best Actor, Best Actress, Best Supporting Actor) TV awards in Kowloon. And we cannot forget that vampires are originally from Europe!

There are two important themes running through the discussion of vampires. First is the idea of a cult following and the second is the belief that vampires are real and live among us today as an outsider culture. Clearly there are elements of the U.S. society who are fascinated with vampires.

And that fascination has led to the formation of a new lifestyle called vampyres – people who during the day are quite ordinary. They may sit next to you in class or even work in the next cubicle, but when the sun goes down, they become creatures of the night.

What do vampyres do? Think of Anne Rice's vampires who are constantly searching for one of their own. Vampyres, then, are constantly looking for other vampyres. And where would they expect to find each other except at clubs catering to the vampyre community. These are nightspots with names such as Long Black Veil in Manhattan where one hears music by groups such as Unto Ashes, Nosferatu, the Shroud, Inkubus Sukkubus and Cruxshadows. The music sounds dirge-like and medieval. Lyrics are not your usual love song:

"After you sink your teeth into my neck
Will you cry out in the passion of the moment
Or writhe around the bed to free yourself?" (The Viper Song)

Mundanes (nonfabulous night people) are discouraged from attending by high entrance fees. The clubs don't want tourists sitting and staring at the vampyres. This is where the vampyres come to meet and relax. Naturally that means drinks such as the Blood Bath, a cocktail made with three parts red wine, one part Chambord (black raspberry liqueur) and a splash of cranberry juice, topped with a maraschino cherry.

Of course, one needs the right clothes. What's the stylish color of choice? Black, of course, but not just black clothes. Black everything – nails, lips, hair, shoes, makeup and clothes – and it's dead black. Remember Dracula? In legend, he was a count, so he was no sloppy dresser. He frequently appeared in a tux (which fits with black) and a cape – a figure of sartorial splendor, which adds to his romantic image. Therefore, one should not be surprised to find that the vampyres are quite well dressed albeit in Edwardian and Victorian clothing – dresses with

33

empire waistlines. Lots of brocades and velvets – not the standard off the rack wear. Thus, one needs to patronize stores such as Religious Sex in the East Village of New York, or Gothic Renaissance. There one can find a black hooded velvet cape with a purple satin lining ($199.95).

These stores also carry the right cosmetics. Along with the black lipstick and nail polish are items such as Pallor Protector (SPF 45) which includes this instruction: "Apply to face and neck before daybreak to avoid the ravages of the sunrise and preserve your preternatural power." For other goodies, try www.vampirecosmetics.com in Los Angeles. Lots of eye makeup, lip treatments and finger nail polishes in black, white, grey and blood-reds. On Amazon.com, one puts goodies in one' shopping cart, but at vampirecosmetics.com, one puts goods in one's shopping coffin. The background for the site is black, the lettering is gothic and there's not much color at the site. But they now have a catalog which is free with a $25 purchase and they have different click sites for U.S. and international customers!

Now what else would vampyres need besides night clubs, music, makeup and clothes? Fangs – yes, they've got to have fangs. For that, there's Transformatorium, where you can get a starting set of two fangs to a full set of all fangs called piranha sets (but it's hard to keep from biting your tongue with those). Fangs are displayed in a glass case and can cost from $75 to $350. Although most popular at Halloween, the shop sells 5 to 10 pairs of fangs a day. All the fang fitters at Transformatorium have some dental training and the fangs are hand-carved out of dental acrylic. The fang-fitting process begins with the fitter taking a cast of your teeth. Once the fangs are carved, the client comes in for a fitting, which can take up to an hour. Once fitted, the fangs stay in place because a groove goes up to the gum line, eliminating the need for adhesive and the fangs can still be pulled off and on.

Transformatorium can also sell you "the look to enhance your inner image" as the Web site says … "whether you're demon, werewolf or vampire." Besides the fangs, there are nails, horns, claws and special contact lenses to erase the whites from your eyes. There is also jewelry (lots of bat-wing earrings), deviant devices (which turns out to be coming soon) and toys for your darker side along with coffin boxes and gothic sacks. In short, nearly all the paraphernalia to become a vampyre.

What else would you need? How about a coffin? For sleeping purposes, or as a coffee table? You can have one custom-made at www.yourcoffin.com. Strangely enough, your coffin is not an exclusively vampire Web site. It is a humorous look at coffins with bikini-clad models and a spoof on getting coffin tobogganing declared an Olympic sport. But you can order your coffin made of mahogany, black oak, pickled oak or several shades of maple, metal or rope handles, with engraved plagues, with shelves – especially wine rack shelves – and a hinged lid. Obviously, sleeping in one's coffin is not the only thing they expect one to use the coffin for.

Vampyre club personnel estimate that there are at least 1,000 vampyres in New York and large groups of vampyres, called clans, exist in Europe, California and Texas (especially Texas). This arising of vampyrism necessitates a need for organizations such as sanguinarium.org, which maintains a nation-wide network of vampire clubs complete with ranks and initiation rites. The goal of Sanguinarium is to unify the vampyre subculture. It has an almanac, magazine, organizes festivals and forums, maintains a directory of international businesses, Web sites, organizations and nightclubs. Sanguinarium has a council with a formal organization of directors and ministers. Among other things C.O.V.I.C.A. (the council) helps to dispel misbeliefs about vampyres. They want you to know that vampyres are not affected by garlic or crosses (indeed their symbol is the ankh which is an Egyptian cross) and do not speak with phony Romanian accents. (If you want to know more, try the FAQ section.)

Then, what are vampyres like? They prefer night to day and are drawn to vampire icons (bats, coffins and capes). They give each other names such as Rapture, Shadow and Kaos. They have terms for various occupations; waitresses are vampiresses and the bartenders are alchemists. Above all, they seem to be interested in body worship and blood worship. They wear fabulous clothes (quite fancy and elaborate), PVC fetish-wear with lots of accessories such as black boots. They get piercings and adorn their bodies with tattoos. According to one observer, "they are celebrating humanity through the blood coursing through their veins." And they are obsessed with seduction in any form. Hence the sexual, sensual and erotic overtones of many vampire movies and Anne Rice's books.

Another observer thinks that people are drawn to vampyrism because of the transcendence of death. They take the worst thing that can happy, dying, and get incredible power out of it. There is a real hunger for the mystical in the movement. One vampyre says "The vampire mystique gives me a sense of empowerment. It lets me pretend to be someone different for a while. It's also a way of having a secret that I share only with those I choose to share it with."

There's also a little rebel among the vampyres. "If you dress up as a vampire, you're challenging everybody's perceptions. People who do this want something a little surreal and they like to experiment," according to Julian Ravage, a semi-retired vamp and director of several New York cable shows.

Are they out of their coffins? Not all are. Some are still quite unwilling to let their co-workers, acquaintances and even parents know that they have adopted the vampyre lifestyle. Thus, they lead two lives, which includes deception and another "world" – all part of the mysticism and romanticism.

Do they drink blood? Not a simple question to answer. Most don't; after all blood is not a pleasing taste. On the other hand, there are those who do want blood and engage in drinking it among a small circle of carefully chosen friends. We are not going to ask what kind of blood.

Are they all bad? Not at all. According to one vampyre, they are definitely not out to hurt people. Some vampyre organizations have even donated cases of school supplies to charities for children and at Christmas, they gave away 20 cases of toys to a group called Toys for Tots.

Of course, there are no real vampires, are there? Along the edges of the vampyre community are rumors and intimations of individuals who claim to be the real thing – murderous, immortal and predatory. Some claim to be 400 years old. In 1996, a young reporter, Susan Walsh, disappeared while investigating the vampire underworld and her case has never been solved. So, who knows?

Questions for Discussion:

1. Are vampyres a legitimate subculture? (Use the terminology associated with subcultures in your textbook to answer this question.)
2. Are vampyres a lifestyle?
3. Is there a relationship between lifestyles and subcultures? If so, what is it?
4. How does business support lifestyles and cater to subcultures?
5. Why is the internet such a popular information and vending medium for vampyres?
6. Vampyres are frequently associated with wicca, which can be found on many college campuses. See if you can find a vampire or witch to interview. How are they part of a subculture or lifestyle? Is it similar to what's described in the case?

7. Are there other businesses or services that could be offered to vampyres?
8. How could major cosmetic companies cater to this segment without damaging their image with the overall market?

References:

Altner, Patricia, "A Coven of Vampires," <u>Library Journal</u>, v. 123, n 12. P139 (2).

Flint, Joe, "Would Buffy Ever Desert the WB and Jump to Fox?" <u>Wall Street Journal</u>, March 11, 2001, p. B1 & B6.

Manning, Toby, "Prime-time eroticism," <u>New Statesman & Society</u>, January 20, 1995, v. 8, n. 336, p. 31(2).

Mittelbach, Margaret and Michael Crewdson, "To Die For: Painting the Town Red, and the Capes and Nails Black," <u>The New York Times</u>, November 24, 2000, E13.

Moesch, Christine, "Piercing the Darkness: Undercover with vampires in America Today," <u>Library Journal</u>, September 15, 1998, v. 123, n. 15, p. 97.

Wong, Sharon, "Night of the vampires," <u>New Straits Times</u>, April 11, 1999, p. 748.

Softening, Polishing and Coloring the Male Market

It's the weekend beauty ritual. Need to touch up those roots with some Feria and try that new facial scrub and moisturizer? Got some new body scrub, Rainforest, that comes with a coarser cloth? That ought to take off those dry skin cells! Gonna style my hair, spritz on the mist and I'm outta' here. Oops! Can't forget to shave.

Yep....shave. We're not talking a female beauty ritual, this is a male ritual for the weekend. It probably caught you off guard and maybe you're wondering "What kind of guy..." or maybe it sounds good to you. Chances are that your father wouldn't be caught dead doing this, but you or his grandsons might. Of course, lots of celebrities such as Freddy Mercury, Dennis Rodman, Lenny Kravitz and Quentin Tarrentino have worn male cosmetics for years, but many of them were doing it more for shock effect than as a matter of good grooming, comfort or enjoyment.

King Gillette started a revolution when he and his partner, a gentlemen with the last name of Nickerson, introduced the safety razor. (One of the ironies of fate is that the company is named for Gillette who actually did very little with it compared to Nickerson, who was really the founding manager, but who had a most unfortunate name for a shaving business.) Sales of the safety razor got off to a slow start in the first years of this century and might have languished for decades had not two events occurred. The first was the endorsement of the Gillette safety razor by baseball great Honus Wagner. Second, the U.S. government gave safety razors to soldiers during World War I. Not only did that speed adoption by U.S. men, but also introduced the safety razor to Europe. To this day, Gillette has significant sales in Europe.

The safety razor was important because it got men to shave. Of course, men shaved and groomed before it, but only in pain as they scraped those facial hairs off with a straight razor. Of course that agony could be mitigated somewhat by going to the barber, but even so, it's no wonder that there were so many bearded men in the nineteenth century.

The safety razor not only made shaving more comfortable, but also easier and faster which encouraged men to pay more attention to their appearance. *And most importantly*, it left their faces uncovered, thereby stimulating the need for facial treatments. To begin with, there was shaving cream (in soap blocks and aerosols in the 1950s), then after shave (mid-twentieth century) and today there's Gillette's Pacific Light Moisturizing After Shave Splash with a non-stinging formula developed for sensitive-skin users. Throughout the twentieth century, the shaving ritual has stimulated (albeit slowly) the use of skin care products. The use of after shave lotions not only helped to "seal" the skin after shaving but also acclimated men to using scented products. Using cologne is only a small step away from-after shave lotions and bracers.

Fragrances

The first companies to sell men's "colognes" used branded products such as Old Spice and Mennen aimed squarely at the male market – not to be confused with women's products. Then, in the last quarter of the century, the men's cologne market went up scale with designed fragrances from the likes of Calvin Klein and Hugo Boss, but these were still clearly men's products. Eventually, a few companies introduced unisex colognes such as Versace's Hello and Calvin Klein's CK One. These were followed by twinned fragrances such as Arrogance for You (men) and Arrogance for Me (women) from Schiapparelli Pikenz, and Eurocosmesi's Light Him and Light Her. Designers also entered the twinned fragrance market with entries like DKNY Men and DKNY Women; LizSport (women) and Claiborne Sport (men); and Tommy Hilfiger's Tommy (men) and Tommy for Women.

Selling colognes and fragrances to men is no simple task, as the rollout of Envy for Men illustrates. Gucci began the rollout in its free-standing boutiques in Italy and the U.S. This was followed by introductions in major department stores such as Saks Fifth Avenue, Bloomingdales', Nordstrom, and Neiman Marcus in the U.S., and in other countries: Germany, the U.K., France and Scandinavia, Japan, Australia and Southeast Asia, including China and South Korea. Between January and December, the product was placed in 1,100 stores.

The rollout was supported with a $40 million promotional budget. The print campaign was shot in black and white by fashion photographer Mario Testino and starred models Jason Fedele and Georgina Grenville. It was shot in Los Angeles because the company wanted an urban setting with hard light. Sales promotions included plastic spray samples in European perfumeries and miniature bottles to be given away to regular customers. In the U.S., 40 million cards affixed with Scent Seal samples were distributed in stores along with vial-on-card samples and miniature fragrances.

To appeal to men, Gucci also invested heavily in packaging. Envy for men came in a chunky rectangular bottle with a black Lucite cap. It was encased in two pieces of black Styrofoam under shrink-wrapped plastic. The Styrofoam casing didn't quite close, which enabled one to peek at the liquid, which is a deeper green than Envy for Women. According to Tom Ford, Gucci's creative director, "We developed that beautiful acidy green, and we didn't want to hide that in a box." For the bottle, he wanted a shape that "would sit well in a man's hand." "Everything that inspires me is 20th Century, and Bauhaus influenced everyone. It's all about lines and planes. I wanted to make a bottle that was strong and sharp and direct and would look beautiful in our new stores. The idea is modern luxury, minimal in the lines, but not in materials."

Designer fragrances have been important in unlocking the men's cosmetics market. They are a natural extension to achieving the designer look of Calvin Klein, Hilfigure, and Versace clothing. The fragrances are supposed to complement the clothing lines so that the man has the complete designer package.

While designer fragrances penetrate the male market at the higher end ($40 to $60+ for Envy for Men), Mary Kay cosmetics has designs on the middle market with their Domain line ($18 to $34). "The Domain concept truly talks about a guy who is very set on the direction in his life. He has things in balance. He is very down-to-earth and believes in commitment. People enjoy being around him," said Lisa Cohorn, director of product marketing at Mary Kay. "It is very aspirational."

Domain was geared to the 30- to 55 year old market and signals Mary Kay's serious approach to the male cosmetics market. Domain is to be followed by a scent aimed at younger men. "We just have as a company really realized the strong potential the men's market has. We are ready to focus on the men's market," commented Cohorn.

To support the launch of Domain, Mary Kay departed from its pink Cadillac incentive program in favor of two Denali sport utility vehicles – one for a sales associate and one for a customer. In addition, there was print advertising, banner ads on the Internet and gift-with-purchase offers of a men's toiletries bag that contained trial sizes of other Mary Kay men's items. It was introduced first in the U.S., then Canada, Europe and Mexico. Within seven months, it was available to male consumers around the globe.

Hair Care Products

In the early part of the century, men also began to pay more attention to their hair as well as their faces. Hair pomades became popular for corralling short hair so that it didn't flop into one's face. Remember shots of Valentino and other silent movie stars with those plastered-down locks? Or did you see "Oh Brother Where Art Thou" in which George Clooney proclaimed himself a Dapper Dan man because of his heavy use of Dapper Dan hair dressing?

By the 1960s, however, hair dressings were falling out of favor as men sought a more natural look. Indeed, men of that era were chided for wearing what was called "greasy, kid stuff." As men let their hair grow longer, they began to blow dry it like their mothers, girlfriends and wives. From there, it was a small step to hair spray and other hair care products such as Grecian Formula for covering the gray.

The advertising for Grecian Formula illustrates two major characteristics of the older male cosmetics user. They want to do whatever the treatment is at home and they don't want anyone to know that they're doing it. Grecian formula ads showed endless men in front of their medicine cabinet mirrors combing Grecian formula through their ever-darkening hair (one of the attractions of lapsed time photography). The ads stressed over and over that you weren't dying your hair, just revitalizing the natural color and that no one would ever know. Sort of strains one's credulity, doesn't it, to believe that *no one* would ever notice. It's important to realize how much reinforcement men needed to take this first step toward dying their hair.

Many young men today have no such inhibitions. College and high school classrooms are filled with guys who do their locks with home use products such as Feria or B Blonde for Men. There's no hiding a color transformation when it's a bleached rather than a dyed look. Last summer when Clairol ran a promotional event to sell hair bleaches, so many guys showed up that the company ran out of water. L'Oreal's Feria has been a very pleasant surprise as it has greatly exceeded the company's expectations – so much so that they're now working on facial washes and moisturizers to expand its product offerings to young guys.

Hair coloring for men has also moved out of the bathroom as more men go out to have their hair done. Toni & Guy is a chain of 220 salons that sell their own hair care line under the brand name Tigi. The names of these products make it clear that they're for guys and young guys at that with items like "Bed Head Manipulator, which is a tub of sticky blue cream that retails for $16.95. The labeling reinforces the name with phraseology such as "a funky gunk that rocks." Then, there's Bed Head Power Trip, a hair gel for $11.95. Noticeably none of this is cheap. A cut and color may cost as much as $95.00. For the more adventurous, there's services such as "a shoeshine" where a stylist colors just the tips of the hair. It should also be pointed out that many men have abandoned the barbershop for styling salons that cater to both sexes.

One of the more interesting hair products for men is hair gel. As noted previously, heavy hairdressings and pomades virtually disappeared from the American scene in the 1960s. Today's product (gel) is lighter and designed for men to sculpt rather than plaster down their hair. In the U.S. and U.K., gel users tend to be younger, but in Latin and South American countries, hair gel has long been a popular product with men of all ages.

Skin Care for Men

The skin care market for men is really beginning to take off. "This has been a long time coming," says Aramis Vice President of Product Development Worldwide Matt Teri, "and it's here to stay." Teri attributes much of this growth to the resurgence of the health and fitness craze, athletic clubs and cosmetic surgery. He believes that today's man is increasingly susceptible to male-specific magazines, new retailing concepts, and launches of new male products. In particular, he thinks that unisex products have encouraged men to try a broader range of toiletries. "Today, men are a lot more in tune with improving their looks and trying a lot of products in both the men's and women's arenas," he said.

In late 2000, Aramis launched a new men's line, "Surface" with the tagline, "Look your best in an instant." The line consists of Shine Erasing Gel, Instant Correcting Stick, Optimizing Skin Gel, Skin Smoothing Gel and Healthy Look Gel and was developed with men's wants in mind. According to Teri, men want products with immediate benefits and that go on very dry, smooth and quickly. They also want comfort which is why the Skin Smoothing Gel teats the texture of the skin with elastomer technology to make the product feel dry and weightless when applied.

Men need their own skin care products because what works for the girlfriend isn't right for men's thicker skin. It has more blood vessels and capillaries close to the surface and more oil production. So, Aramis designed "Surface" to combat shine and tone down redness. It has a lighter weight texture because men don't want anything heavy or occlusive on their skin. Teri thinks that it must be light and feel invisible to appeal to the male customer.

Mary Kay also has a line of male skin care products called Skin Management for Men. It includes Cooling Toner, Blemish Control Formula, Enriched Shave Cream, Conditioner with Sunscreen and Oil Controller with Sunscreen. Carol Margolis, director of product marketing for skin care, body care, fragrance and diet supplements at Mary Kay, said that the "research we did told us that in some ways what men want from skin-care products parallels what women want: simple, routine, multi-benefit products. Yet, men have their own needs, too. They're looking for non-fragranced skin care; they want to feel fresh without the fragrance."

Both Surface and Skin Care Management for Men have manly packaging and ad campaigns that highlight technology and products as tools. While Mary Kay's products focus on repairing and protecting the appearance of the skin, the Aramis products go a step further by utilizing optical illusion and color cosmetics to improve a man's visage. Optimizing Skin Cream has blue reflectors and mirror spheres that work to neutralize redness; the product immediately counteracts ruddiness on the skin," said Teri. "It plays with light and the color of the skin to create the illusion of younger, healthier skin."

What about color cosmetics? Surface's Healthy Look Gel adds a rush of color to pale skin. Recognizing that men wouldn't use a blusher, Teri commented that Aramis took the concept of a bronzer (which men are more comfortable with), sheered out the color and gave it a neutral tonality that works for any man's complexion. It's applied differently as no brush is used. The Instant Correcting Stick also incorporates the blue reflectors and is dubbed a "fix-it" stick so that the guys can fix under-eye circles and broken capillaries without using a woman's concealer. It's in a Chapstick-type container because men are used to using Chapstick.

What's next at Aramis? Teri suggested a product for getting rid of unibrow, body products and more color cosmetics along with line extensions for Surface. He plans to stick to discrete improvements.

The experience of BeautiControl indicates that not all men are ready to adopt the use of skin care products. By re-positioning its Skin Strategies line from skin care to a men's shaving care line, it increased sales by 5 percent. The dove gray packaging of the skin care line was replaced with black packaging featuring simple lettering. Products were renamed. The Skin Cleanser became a Pre-Shave Cleansing Gel; the Exfoliating Scrub is now a Beard Lifting Scrub and a Soothing Moisturizer is renamed Soothing After Shave Balm. Only Revitalizing Eye Gel remained the same. Hard to tie eye gel to shaving! Gary Jones, vice president of product development, commented that "Men have the same concerns (as women), but we haven't been programmed to indulge in our own vanity…So our goal was, to look at the routine that a man has every day. We were not asking him to alter that routine, but we designed the line of products to fit into that… We realized that men are fickle and funny about skin care products…We don't use a moisturizer, but we will use an aftershave balm." He also noted that men don't want to have to ask how to use it. So, Skin Strategies makes simple, easy to use products and planned to introduce a fragrance in the future.

Sunscreens are another skin care product where male lines are being introduced. Brad Beirman was exhibiting his company's sun protection products when a man grabbed him by the elbow and asked "Got anything a man can use?" Like most men, he was tired of sunscreens that felt heavy as maple syrup and smelled like tropical fruit. Six months later, he was wearing Bierman's oil-free, unscented, waterproof SmartShield product line, which includes sunscreen lotions for skin, eyelids and lips.

Observers believe that men are more willing to buy skin care products because unisex stores such as the Gap and Banana Republic have introduced their own skin care lines. Men are comfortable shopping at these stores and the presence of the male cosmetic products indicates that it's all right for men to care about their appearance.

That's skin care. What about soaps? In mid-2000, Procter & Gamble introduced a Zest body wash aimed at guys in their teens and twenties. The company picked Zest because it has traditionally been popular with males. It used bright primary colors on the packages and names like Rainforest Adventure and Energy Rush. They eliminated the pouf (mesh ball) sold with women's products and substituted a mesh cloth that is rougher than a regular wash cloth.

The International Male Cosmetics Scene

While men in the U.S. are cleansing, dying and spraying scents, what about men in the rest of the world? Here's just a sprinkling of insights. In Europe, the number of men using facial skincare/cleansing products weekly rose by 19% in the early to mid-nineties. The percentage of men using moisturizer grew by nearly 4.5 %. L'Oreal data in the mid-nineties reveal that 32% of German men claimed to use a facial moisturizer, compared with 25% of U.K. men, 24% of French men, and 18% of Italian men. The French man was noted for being more likely to incorporate skin care products into his daily grooming routine than were U.K. and Italian men.

Asian men have begun to realize that their appearance is important. Consequently, beauty salons throughout Asia offer dozens of treatment programs for male executives. Among them are relaxing massages and facials, non-surgical face-lifts and laser removal of facial hair.

The Japanese, male cosmetics market was 200 billion yen in 1998 and men's facial creams have become one of the fastest-selling products. Young Japanese men in particular tend to have a keen sense of beauty and cleanliness. For them, Shiseido has introduced Naturgo Men's Clay Sengan Form which is a facial scrub containing natural clay from the Alps. It is sold with a twin product, Clay Pack, and has been a big hit according to Shiseido personnel. Sales have reached 200,000 units per month. Other companies such as Mandom Corporation have also released facial products such as Facial Clay Wash made from sea clay.

In Brazil, sales of men's cosmetics rose by 30% and sales of perfumes rose by 24% in the late 1990s. According to industry statistics, 21% of men use skin care products. Major brands are Shiseido's Basala which grew at 25%, Natura and L'Oreal. Sales are so good that Avon is expanding its sales force in Brazil.

Who's the Market?

There is an obvious split in the men's cosmetics market. Older men (middle age and over) may be willing to use some skin care products and colognes, but the more out-there products like the hair bleaches and heavy duty skin care products are aimed at younger men – especially teens.

The teens are not only willing to try new products, but they are much more willing to be seen buying and using the products. But they are a hard market to reach. Gillette can advertise to older men on television and designer fragrances and products can advertise to the same men in *GQ*.

But where do advertisers go to reach young men? Two publishers think that they have the answer. TransWorld Media, a unit of Tribune Co., has launched Stance, a magazine with a raunchy bent. Rodale Inc. launched a spinoff of its Men's Health magazine for teen guys entitled *MH-18*. The former publication (*Stance*) counted on babes to attract the guys – just like its big brother publications, *Maxim, Gear,* and *FHM*. According to the publisher, "It's a combination of things that teenage boys want to look at: girls, sports, gear, music – and girls."

MH-18, on the other hand, tried a softer approach with articles on topics like how to boost grades, workout plans, and girl-kissing tips although its editor promises to stay away from all those exclamation points in girls magazines. For its initial cover, it passed out photos to teen boys in focus groups. The groups rejected one guy as "too sweet" and another as too serious. Then there was the issue of a shirt – should the model wear one? Focus groups were split on this, so the editors bravely went for the shirtless model and plastered an article for an Ideal 8-Week Body Workout across his chest.

Both publishers claimed to have had no trouble attracting advertisers among the likes of Calvin Klein, Sony, Skechers U.S.A., Unionbay and Nestle's – a lineup of clothiers, electronics and candy. When one considers that there are about 16 million boys age 12 to 19 in the U.S. and they spend an average of $101 per week, this looks like a winner of a market. On the other hand, previous publishers have failed to capture the boys' attention for very long. Maybe they'd rather read their big brother's mags.

Would these guys respond to ads for cosmetics? Some definitely would. At one of <u>MH-18's</u> focus groups, the guys asked for "those smelly pages." It took the magazine's director a moment (or two) to realize that they were asking for perfume ads with scent strips.

What's Next?

If the young guys are the market – open and willing to try new products and they're already bleaching their hair and using moisturizers and scents, what could be sold to them next? A company named Hard Candy thinks it has the answer – nail polish. In the late 1990s, it launched a new line called Hard Candy with polishes aimed at the male market. Colors included Testosterone (metallic silver), Dog (deep purple), Oedipus (forest green), Gigolo (black with silver accents), Superman (a sparkly midnight blue) and Libido (a metallic teal) which were sold in department starts and men's boutiques nation-wide. Company personnel noted that men want darker colors. Although some celebrities have painted their nails, most men have shunned nail polish and color cosmetics in general.

Then, Urban Decay (another cosmetics company) noticed a lot of guys using their polishes aimed at the women's market and introduced a line of guy-friendly colors with names like Uzi (gunmetal gray), Asphalt (silver-speced black), Spare Change (metallic silver) and Chains (antique gold) with profit-producing results. Urban Decay's success spurred Hard Candy to introduce their line. Even a mainstream company like OPI introduced colors for guys – Matte Nail Envy (a modest buff color).

Why would guys wear nail polish? Well, it's one way to differentiate one's self from the crowd and then again, if the rest of your peers are doing it, it's a way to fit in. Other guys find that it's easier to pick up women – gives them something to talk about. Or maybe they're just rebelling or expressing themselves.

At prices of $12.00 per .45 ounce bottle, this is not an inexpensive trend. And it's sheer tedium to file, buff, remove cuticle, apply base coat, two coats of color and a topcoat. Are they going to watch TV talk shows while they wait for it to dry? Even with these drawbacks, the new for-men colors flew off the shelves of stores like Neiman Marcus and John Allen's in New York. Besides the fashion-forward guys, there are others buying the nail polishes. High school coaches across the U.S. have ordered dozens of bottles in school colors for football players to wear on game day. Well, it's a start!

Older men may be more susceptible to wearing polish than we realize. One retailer tells of a middle-aged Beverly Hills stockbroker who paints his toes, but only shows his wife. Are there others out there hiding their painted nails under socks? According to Wende Zomnir of Urban Decay, men need to be gradually introduced to new grooming concepts. "Toenails are a first step for many of our customers. It's like a Bull Durham thing – they know it's there, so they feel good, but no one else can see it," she says. And what about the number of men in salons getting their nails manicured weekly – many of whom have a coat of clear enamel applied to their nails. Maybe the next step is OPI's buff colored polish with a gradual work-up to Gigolo.

According to Dale Crichton, vice president and central merchandise manager for cosmetics at Norstrom, nail polish is "more of a lark for young guys at this stage, but it could develop into something." However, to be successful selling nail polish or other color cosmetics to guys, he says retailers will have to make it easy for guys to find – that they're not going to search through the aisles of the cosmetics department looking for it. Also, he adds, it has to be in the right markets.

Perhaps this unwillingness of guys to be spotted stalking the aisles of cosmetics departments accounts for the fact that one-third of purchasers of cosmetics on the Internet are men. That's more than the one fifth who usually purchase in department stores. Of course, the percentages increase when men can shop in an all-male environment. The rest, which is over half of the either borrows their wives', girlfriends' or female others' products or lets the women buy for them.

This means marketers of male cosmetics have their hands full convincing guys to try new products, to actively shop for them and in finding ways to reach them with advertising. That's why you can't count on seeing lots of painted nails at the gym any time soon.

Questions for Discussion

1. What motivations do men have for using cosmetics? Divide these into rational and emotional and discuss which are the most important in stimulating purchase.
2. How do men learn about cosmetics?
3. How does marketing for male products differ from women's? Try contrasting the marketing by type of product (hair, skin care, fragrances, etc.) Why is the marketing different?
4. How can the concept of self be related to the use of male cosmetics?
5. How can personality and lifestyle be related to the use of male cosmetics?
6. How can marketers convince men to adopt the use of products such as color cosmetics? Are these true innovations?
7. Are products like color cosmetics subject to social group influences? If so, why and how do group influences affect the adoption of these products?
8. How could advertisers attempt to change men's attitudes toward those color cosmetics like the Aramis Healthy Gel Toner and Hard Candy's nail polish?
9. Where and how would you market a line of men's color cosmetics? Think about the tips on marketing to men provided by Crichton at the end of the case.

References

-----, "The Bleach Boys," <u>Chemist & Druggist</u>, Jan. 30, 1999, p. 11 (1).

-----, "Men go mad for facials," <u>Cosmetics International</u>, Feb.10, 1999, v 23, I 514, p 4(1).

-----, "Brazil: men's cosmetics sales grow," <u>South American Business Information</u>, August 9, 1999, p. 10082.

Aktar, Alev, "Donna Karan's Scent of the City," <u>WWD</u>, September 10, 1999, p. 6.

Barone, Amy, "From the chic to the bizarre," <u>WWD</u>, May 2, 1997, v 173, n 85, n 4 (2).

Edwards, Tamala, "Love your nails, Jack," <u>Time</u>, Oct. 6, 1997, v 150, n 14, p 71 (1).

Fine, Jenny B., "Hard Candy gets sweet on men," <u>WWD</u>, January 10, 1997, v 173, n7 p 6 (1).

Forden, Sara Gay and Amy Barone, "Gucci's Envy encore," <u>WWD</u>, January 16, 1998, v 175, n 10, p 6 (1).

Gove, John, <u>Made in America</u>, Berkley Books, New York, NY, 2001.

Klepacki, Laura, "Beauticontrol Courts Men," <u>WWD</u>, Feb. 26, 1999, p. 10 (1).

Klepacki, Laura, "Mary Kay Adds Men to Fragrance Plans," <u>WWD</u>, Feb. 18, 200, p. 8.

Larson, Soren, "Claiborne to try the sporting life," <u>WWD</u>, March 14, 1997, v 173, n 50, p 6 (11).

Marcus, Mary Brophy, "Lotion for dudes: skin cancer protection," <u>U.S. News & World Report</u>, June 16, 1997, v 122, n 23, n 67 (1).

Matthews, Imogen, "Baby bomers turned male groomers," <u>Manufacturing Chemist</u>, Feb. 1997, v 68, n 2, pS24 (2).

Mulrine, Anna, "For the truly polished man," <u>U.S. News & World Report</u>, June 9, 1997, v 122, n 22, p 13 (1).

Nelson, Emily, "Makers of Beauty Products Go Where the Boys Are," <u>Wall Street Journal</u>, August 10, 2000, p. B1 and B5.

Strickland, Sarah, "Narcissus, after all, was a man," <u>Asian Business (Hong Kong)</u>, August 1999, v 35, i 8, p. 54 (2).

Tennerelli, Mary Jane, "Men's Skin Care 2001," <u>Global Cosmetic Industry</u>, March 2001, v 168, I 3, p 22.

CASE
6

The Mundane, Knowne and Fantasy Worlds

You … have … been … weighed … *Thack*… measured…*Ka-bam*… and found wanting! *Double smack!!!!!* Thus, sneers the evil Count Adhemar to our hero, Ulrich von Lichtenstein of Gelderland -- as he slugs the defenseless Ulrich who is bound to a board in prison. It's too much – a beating like this before poor Ulrich who is really … *alas* … commoner William Thatcher is publicly humiliated in the stocks (stocks at that period of time?). Fortunately for our hero, the future King of England finds and knights him before a crowd of commoners who cease throwing cabbages and stones at Ulrich/William and shift to blowing him kisses and cheering him on. Once knighted, William (now Sir William) returns to the jousting field where he defeats the evil count without aid of armor or strength in his arm (*most incredible).*

As the count's just reward, William's squires, who include figures such as Geoff Chaucer, are finally able to tell the Count (you guessed it) you have been weighed, measured and found wanting while the Count is flat on his back after William sent him flying – an outcome that William threatened the Count with throughout the movie and finally, to our delight and none too soon, delivered on.

Seems pitiful little retribution to me for what poor William endured, but then William's blind father gets to hear the crowd scream "Sir William, Sir William Thatcher," William gets the beauteous maiden, Jocelyn and changes his stars by becoming a lord. All this accompanied by a thundering opening of "We Will Rock You" with the crowd doing a medieval wave to a closing of "We are the Champions" (Queen -- good name for a medieval rock group) with lashings of AC/DC, Sly and the Family Stones and David Bowie in between.

While critics sneer worse than Count Adhemar (who was thoroughly despicable) at the inept campiness of the much heralded movie, "A Knight's Tale" ("not as good as Python's anarchic spirit or wit and definitely not satirical enough" according to *Newsweek*), audiences seemed to have loved it. Same story that we've seen again and again (poor hero conquers all the injustices aimed at him and gets the girl, gold, and glory at the end), but this one is wrapped in medieval lore of chivalry, romance, nobility, humor and just plain justice triumphing which may be enough for an escapist afternoon at the flicks.

For some folks, however, an escapist afternoon at the flicks is not enough. This medieval stuff really appeals to them, and therefore, they spend their spare time fashioning swords from rattan sticks wrapped in that most useful of products – silver duct tape, making shields of heavy cardboard or plastic and (you guessed it again) duct tape and helmets of old coffee pots or for larger heads, shrimp cookers. Others spend their time weaving, spinning, fluting and luting (plucking strings, not stealing) and even making their own mead – all in the name of re-creating the medieval period. They make their own costumes. Ladies adopt long gowns with wimples and guys wear tunics that often bear their coat of arms. They learn to do battle with swords, maces and other archaic implements of war – even pikestaffs. Others learn to sing and dance in order to stage fairs and banquets. Some even make their own armor. One of our locals fashions chain mail by winding 16-gauge galvanized steel wire around a metal dowel rod and then weaves the links together with his fingers and pliers. And still others are poets.

Who would do this? The members of the *Society for Creative Anachronism*, known as the SCA. The first time I saw members of this group, about twenty-five of them were staging a mock battle in the local forest theater which is a small open-air theater surrounded most appropriately by -- trees. Although they were only about sixty feet away, we could barely see the fighters through the foliage, but we could hear them yelling things like "For Sir Gawain!" For a moment there, we were transported to a glade in Merrie Olde England and thoughts of Gweneviere, Ivanhoe, and Camelot rushed through our brains. All the scene lacked was mist swirling around those warriors, but then I noticed the pot handle sticking out the back of one foot soldier's homemade helmet.

For the SCA, the Knowne Worlde is divided into thirteen kingdoms that employ among other occupations, cartographers who spend their time making maps that define the kingdoms. The kingdoms have names like Drachenwald, or my favorite the kingdom of Ansteorra (which means Lone Star in Anglo-Saxon and incorporates present-day Texas and Oklahoma). Within each kingdom is an intricate mosaic of shires, baronies, duchies, principalities, cantons and households, some conforming to real geography, others existing only in the minds of a given group or on the Internet.

Members of the SCA can adopt any period or persona they choose from any culture in the world between AD 500 and 1600. For example, the Honourable Lady Gwillian ferch Maredudd, a 14th century Welch woman, is really a cultural anthropologist at St. Edward's University in Austin, Texas named Wendy Erisman in what Society members call the "mundane world, or Mundania." (Frequently, all too right!)

Maps are used to deconflict shire boundaries. Deconflict? Unhappily not. Thus, SCAdians spend weekends in battles which tend to culminate in major wars attended by SCAdians from around the world. At these pre-organized wars, fighters join whichever side their local baron has chosen – the alliances having been brokered on the Internet, telephone or simply on the whim of the day.

That is why 9,000 SCAdians gathered recently in Western Pennsylvania to fight the Pennsic War. It began when the kings of the East and Middle Kingdoms marched onto the battlefield to break a ceremonial arrow and ended after "days" of battle. The two armies – each 1,500 strong – marched onto the field and at a cannon shot rushed at each other screaming, rattan swords waving in the air and spears striking shields. When struck a killing blow, combatants are honor-bound to fall, or to fight one-armed or kneeling should a limb be lost. Quickly, bodies littered the field. When marshals cried "Hold," the action stopped so the dead could walk to safety and attendants could dole out water and Gatorade. The battle ended within 45 minutes of stops and starts when the Easterners slayed the last opponent. "They died too quickly," says Lord Dieterich, aka Jordan Weinstein (a computer science student in Manhattan). But it's just one battle. The East does go on to win the entire war and wins the coveted prize: bragging rights until next year. They get to keep the disputed territory and the losers get Pittsburgh.

Of course, there are rules of battle. One's equipment must meet minimum standards; one must know how to use the equipment and to perform as a foot soldier or whatever along with knowing when to kneel or "die." Everyone winds up with bruises and occasionally a broken limb because it *does* hurt to be hit with a rattan stick which, no doubt, accounts for the purchase of professionally-made armor by some members.

Started in California (where else?) forty years ago, SCA has re-invented medieval culture and sent it back from whence it came. It has chapters all across the U.S., throughout Europe, Australia, New Zealand, South Africa and non-Anglo type countries such as Japan, Greece and Turkey. Great Britain is actually one of the newer additions and Scandinavians are enjoying re-pillaging it all over again. Thus, the Pennsic War was more of a global affair than any battle ever fought in medieval times.

Why would people spend their weekends and vacations this way? Stress relief, possibly. "I think it's because they have to sit at a desk doing computer programming, so they like to get out on the weekends and schwack on people. It's quite a stress reliever. You put on all that armor and start schwacking on each other. There's nothing like it, believe you me," says one enthusiastic participant.

"It's a good way to meet people," adds a local electrical engineer and "it looks like fun being able to hit people with sticks," says one SCAdian's eleven-year old son who is hoping they'll start a junior league of SCA.

Some are more interested in the medieval crafts and learning. For example, two SCA scientists, Peter Manly and Daniel Smith, observed Jupiter, Saturn and the crescent phases of Venus through recreations of Galileo's wooden telescopes made to the Florentine's original design and mounted on simple wooden tripods. Like other members of SCA guilds, these two men routinely display their research at public events and schools. Remember Lady Gwillian ferch Maredudd? In the mundane world, she wrote her PhD thesis on the SCA and describes it as an international community "imagined in the appropriation of space and time by mapping a group geography and developing a communal history and tradition."

For some, it's simply nostalgia, which seems to be raging throughout our lives. We are surrounded by people driving the "new" bug, listening to the Eagles, buying Boxsters, eating Necco wafers (19th century candy), and going to baseball in "old" stadiums like Camden Yard. Advertisers are dusting off old slogans such as "Good to the last drop (Maxwell House)" and Charlie the Tuna is back. When they paired James Brown's "I feel good" with Senokot laxatives, that was going too far.

They keep trying to revive bell-bottoms because nostalgia sells. Just look at the popularity of Victoria magazine, movies such as *Mansfield Park*, *Sense and Sensibility*, and the growth of antique malls. We are a nation looking to the past. Main Street in Disney World is, after all, kind of Victorian, and Cinderella's castle is …well, a castle, and Disney capitalizes on knights, sleeping beauties, dwarfs and other fairy tales. Retro marketing not only copies the past but also brings it back (use of actual black and white footage from the fifties) and updates it. The little girl shown in the old Shake'n'Bake or Kool-Aid ads now appears grown up after dreaming of her mother's kitchen at the beginning of the ad.

But this is nostalgia with a difference. Yes, the SCA tries to be authentic, but it is actually more creative, freer than the medieval world was or even the mundane world is today. Comments one female SCAdian, "If we were really going to accurately recreate the Middle Ages, there would be no freedom for women. But any man who wants me to be subservient has a nasty shock coming."

Actually, it makes for a better world. One observer writes "By recreating the xenophobia and aggression of the medieval world, but at the same time taking the suffering out, the SCA has unwillingly created an international subculture of tolerance, communication and play. Real geography is transcended. The real world, 'Mundania,' is put on hold. Which brings us back to where we began – day dreaming about a more ideal world."

Is this why some of our locals re-enact a Revolutionary War battle at a nearby park or others participate in Civil War Re-enactments? Do women harbor desires to be Southern Belles? Do men want to be heroes on the battlefield? Do they want to re-write history? Re-interpret the world? Return to honor or chivalry? Create a new world? Do we want to rise above the mundane world like William Thatcher? Be champions? Rock the World? Or do we just want to slug the count?

Questions for Discussion

1. The three Fs of Consumer Behavior are Feelings, Fantasy and Fun. Do these apply to joining the SCA? In other words, why do people join groups like the SCA, the Civil War re-enactors, modern-day war (paint ball) games participants or even actors in the local theater?

2. A fourth F – how does doing this fulfill our lives?

3. Why would nostalgia sell?

4. How does choosing one's persona relate to self concept? What would you choose if you were in the SCA? Aren't these people branding themselves? How?

5. Myths help to define our culture and are stories containing symbolic elements that express the shared emotions and ideals of the culture. What kind of myths does "A Knight's Tale" contain? What does it say about our culture? If people are drawn to the SCA to re-define the world, what does that say about our real world, Mundania?

6. According to the case, the SCA has created a subculture. How is it a subculture and what differentiates it from other subcultures?

7. What types of local businesses could cater to the SCA? How?

8. Explain the following statement: Fantasy can be big business. What other means are there to providing consumers with fantasy besides the SCA, movies and re-enactments.

References

-----, "For the love of an anachronistic art," <u>Maclean's</u>, Sep 30, 1996, v 109, n 40, p 13(1).

Ansen, David, "Knight Lite: Joust-Add-water formula," <u>Newsweek</u>, May 14, 2001, p. 57.

Johnson, Maria, "Knight Watch," <u>Greensboro News and Record</u>, May 18, 2001, p. D1
(2).

Isaacson, Rupert, "Knights of passion," <u>Geographical</u>, Jan. 2000, v 72, I 1, p 63 (5).

Miller, Kenneth and Bill Eppridge, "A medieval battle," <u>Life</u>, Nov. 1995, v 18, n 13, p 28
(4).

Schickel, Richard, "A Knight's Tale: Directed by Brian Helgeland," <u>Time</u>, May 21,
2001, v 157, I 20, p 92.

Doing Thai Food Right

Overheard in Pung's House of Thai restaurant:

Susan :   "I'd like Yum Nurr, but could you make it mild?"
Waitress: "Certainly. Would you like anything else?"
Susan: "That's it. No. Wait a minute. Does Yum Nurr come with rice?"
Waitress: "No. It's a salad."
Susan: "Well, I would like some rice with it anyway. Can you do that?"
Waitress: "Certainly."

Just a typical restaurant order here in the U.S. – Thai food, but hold the hot and spicy. Many of us here don't like our food Thai-hot, -spicy or -sour. To please U.S. palates, some of those fermented sauce dishes may need a few drops of sugar to tame the strong natural taste.

But just suppose that the following happened….
Susan: "I'd like Yum Nurr, but could you make it mild?"
Waitress: "I'm sorry, but we don't alter dishes. This is an authentic Thai restaurant. Yum Nurr is traditionally spicy. If you would like something less tangy, may I suggest …."

What's Susan going to do now? Make the substitution? Insist on the spicy dish with fewer flames? Or go elsewhere? How will she feel about this experience? Americans and many Europeans are trained to "have it their way" – not some arbitrary food expert's way. Susan may well substitute something this time, but silently vow never to return to this restaurant. What restaurant would insist on serving it their way rather than the customer's anyway?

The answer is Global Thai Restaurants Co. (GTR) initiated by the Thai Government. Happy about the tremendous growth of Thai restaurants world-wide, but unhappy about the alteration of Thai food to suit local tastes, the Thai government plans to support the launch of more than 3,000 restaurants world-wide with more than 1,000 in the U.S. alone. The goal? To ensure that Americans eat genuine Thai food – hot like it's supposed to be or sour like it's supposed to be.

There will be three versions of GTR restaurants. At Golden Leaf restaurants, customers will eat Royal Thai cuisine surrounded by staff in traditional dress and listen to Thai classical music. Dinners there should run in the $25-30 range. Cool Basil restaurants will offer contemporary dining and be located in large shopping malls. Dinner there will be $15-20.

Finally, Elephant Jumps will be fast food restaurants that serve single dish meals costing about $5 to 10.

The restaurants will not, however, be wholly owned and operated by the government. Recognizing that they are unlikely to make good restauranteurs, the government will hold only a 30% interest in the venture with the rest coming from other partner(s). Among the interested companies are Starwood Hotels & Resorts Worldwide of White Plains, NY and AFC Enterprises Inc., of Atlanta and Church's chicken fame. An alternative plan would be to find a master franchiser in each country.

To ensure that the food sold in GTR restaurants is truly authentic, the government's Export Promotion Department is standardizing 200 dishes for inclusion on menus. As a result customers anywhere in the world will get the same dish. To supply the restaurants, the department will help set up food catering centers in different parts of the world. While these will be privately staffed and managed, they will receive raw foodstuffs from Thailand and, in turn, supply semi-cooked foods such as curry. Personnel would be trained in Thailand. The use of catering centers would help to alleviate the shortage of Thai chefs as restaurants would use semi-prepared foods and not need their own chef.

Why is the Thai government so intent on making sure that we eat only proper Thai food? The tremendous demand for Thai food world-wide means more than $6 billion a year from food exports – things such as kaffir-lime leaves and galangal (a gingerlike root) – and more than $1.6 billion from exporting restaurant supplies such as Buddha bronzes and plates. Among the country's fastest growing exports – more than 30% per year – are herbs and spices. The impact on the sluggish and slowly recovering Thai economy does not end with product exports. Thailand exports people such as Thai chefs to countries around the globe. The growth of Thai restaurants has resulted in a shortage of Thai chefs so that cooking schools (also supported by the government) have sprung up in Thailand to fill this need. These schools hold out the hope of striking it rich in the U.S. or Australia for poor Thais. By becoming suppliers and partners of Thai restaurants, the Thai government is trying to assure that some of the riches created by the growth of Thai restaurants return to the home country.

The Thai food craze has also fueled tourism to Thailand. In the year 2000, more than 10 million tourists visited Thailand – more than double the number in 1990. Demonstrating Thailand's new found popularity, it was the setting for Leonardo DiCaprio's much-anticipated follow-up movie to *Titanic*, *The Beach*. The proposed restaurants could be another means of promoting Thailand through posters and travel brochures distributed displayed in the restaurants.

One of the problems, however, of tourists discovering genuine Thai food is that they also learn genuine means of serving it. Rather than the appetizer, salad/soup, main course, dessert parade of restaurants in western countries, Thais usually serve all the foods at once by placing them in the center of the table. In the U.S. that is called *family style* and it means that everyone has to eat the same things and serve themselves. A typical Thai meal has steamed rice, small bowls of clear soup, a steamed dish and a fried dish, a strong sauce usually made with chiles and used for dipping vegetables, and a salad often tossed with meat or fish and tropical fruit for dessert. While that's plenty of variety, there will have to be agreement on the salad and steamed and fried dishes among the diners.

The use of family style raises issues not only of satisfying the tastes of multiple individuals at the same mean, but also the connotations of family style. That is usually reserved for more informal dining which would conflict with the ambiance and price range of the proposed Golden Leaf restaurants.

Another problem is that many Americans perceive ethnic restaurants to be "cheap, little places". The price ranges for most of the GTR restaurants are relatively high and the fast food prices are especially high when compared with $2 hamburgers and less than a $1 tacos. The mass market, which is the domain of the Cool Basil and Elephant Jump restaurants, may expect lower prices.

On the other hand, ethnic foods might benefit from the healthy eating trend – especially the increasing demand for organic vegetables. Given that Thai food emphasizes grains (rice) and vegetables that are not heavily cooked, organic vegetables with their stronger tastes might be more appropriate here. To get variety and eat more healthily, Americans might be willing to pay more.

But will they eat those hot foods? Or only the less spicy ones on the menu? Or will they demand foods cooked their way? Or will they walk out the door?

Questions for Discussion

1. Explain how beliefs, affect and behavior have combined to produce American attitudes toward Thai food? Use your own experience as a guide.
2. How would the introduction of the Thai government's authentic Thai restaurants change the beliefs and affect components of attitude? Then, how might those changes in turn affect behavior?
3. In trying to change consumer attitudes about Thai food, the government will have to establish itself as the message source and communicate a very convincing message. How could the government increase its attractiveness as a source? What kind of message should it use? How could it convey that?
4. In your opinion, will Americans be willing to eat Thai food if they can't have it altered to suit their taste?
5. Indicate how successful you think that the Golden Leaf, Cool Basil and Elephant Jumps restaurants will be? What factors will affect the success of the three types of restaurants?

References

Fabricant, Florence, "The Westernization of Thai food," Nation's Restaurant News, January 3, 1994, v 28, n 1, p 39 (1).

Frank, Robert, "Thai Food for the World?", Wall Street Journal, February 6, 2001, P. B1 & B4.

McCue, Nancy, "Treasures from Thailand," Prepared Foods, May 1996, v 165, n 6, p 101 (2).

Thapanachai, Somporn, "FOOD: Taking Thai restaurants to the world: State will help investors achieve target of eight thousand Thai restaurants abroad in next three years," Bangkok Post, July 27, 2000, p. 12.

Thapanachai, Somporn, "RESTAURANTS: State seen as partner in export venture; Brands tap overseas taste for Thai food," Bangkok Post, December 15, 2000, p. 14.

At the Pump versus Inside the Station

When consumers demanded convenience at the gasoline pump, companies responded with pay-at-the-pump. Just pull into the station, pump your own gas, and pay without ever making the trek into the station. Many consumers seem to have loved the reduction in time and effort that allowed them to get back on the road expeditiously. Sensing a good opportunity to create further consumer convenience, some companies have gone even further. For example, Exxon provides customers with small, portable transponder wands, which they can attach to their key rings. The wand is part of the "Speedpass" system and is preprogrammed with your credit or debit card information. Just wave the wand and you've paid without having to take your credit card from your wallet. (Now if they could just get the nozzle to insert itself and start the gas with a button...) Sound good? Maybe yes for the consumer, but no for the retailer. Thus, other companies are adopting different tactics. Consider the following...

Therese W. of Atlanta recently pulled into her neighborhood gas station and used her credit card to pay at the pump. Instead of just getting a receipt for her credit card purchase, she got coupons on foodstuffs in the station's food shop and for dry cleaning services in the same shopping center.

Welcome to the interactive-merchandising-fuel-pump brought to you through the combined efforts of Marconi Commerce Systems and Edgewater Technology. Strangely enough, these two companies first brought you pay-at-the pump, but now they're bringing you promotion-at-the-pump. Why? Because consumers were no longer going into the store. Why does that matter? The goodies inside the station have higher margins than the gasoline at the pump. Thus, it only made sense for Marconi to now find a way to lure the consumer back inside the station after earlier enabling them to never go into the station.

To determine what consumers might respond to in the form of marketing at the pump, these companies conducted extensive research among women consumers. They found that the women wanted something more than advertising at the pump if the pump was going to communicate with them. According to the female respondents, they get enough advertising elsewhere. Thus the company chose to add value by issuing coupons from nearby retailers. This has high appeal for advertisers because the coupons are printed at the dispenser with a bar code which enables the advertiser to calculate the redemption rate of the coupons in order to determine the effectiveness of the promotions. These pumps are being tested in Atlanta and Marconi has plans to roll them out in 20 major markets in 2001 and into the rest of the country later.

Marconi has high hopes for this technology. If successful, they can use the same software package in beverage dispensers and soda machines as well as stand-alone kiosks for car washes and other locations. Just think. The next time you buy a soda from a machine, you might get a coupon for potato chips. No longer will grocery stores have a monopoly on issuing on-the-spot coupons!

Other companies are even more aggressive at getting the consumer into the gas station. Consider the following scenario…

Recently Rodney O. of Cleveland pulled into a BP station to buy gas. He took his credit card from his wallet to insert in the gas pump and was surprised to find an E-dispenser – a touch and go screen that enabled him to do more than pay for gas. He could pre-order sandwiches and drinks, obtain local news, weather and traffic reports while pumping gas and, of course, pay for the gas! Once he finished pumping the gas, he could go inside to find the hot sandwich (on a croissant) and latte waiting for him. "Way cool," he thought.

Welcome to Site Management – an attempt to generate maximum revenues and profits through a combination of gasoline and soft goods marketing! BP calls this new concept **BP Connect** and BP is willing to bet a bundle on it to overcome a major problem of gasoline retailing. Gasoline is a commodity. We can smell it, don't want to taste or see it, and usually take on faith that the whirring sound at the pump indicates that the stuff is actually going into our cars. Attempting to convince consumers to prefer one gasoline brand over another by advertising additives, tigers, or men with stars has proved to be very difficult, if not impossible. Even gasoline credit cards do not tie customers to a brand of gasoline.

Hence, companies like BP, which recently bought Amoco are working hard to improve their brand image. Starting with the stations, they are using brighter colors, bigger buildings, new logos such as the BP white, yellow and green sunburst, offering a wider array of higher quality foodstuffs and drinks and providing free information such as weather and traffic reports.

BP opened three new **BP Connect** stations in 2000 and planned to roll out 300 more stations to customers in the U.S., the U.K. and Australia in 2001. The largest **BP Connect** sites will be more than 4,200 square feet. They are open and airy and have many shelves limited to waist height. They feature the *Wild Bean Café* and are divided into five sections: food, beverages, impulse-buying such as snacks, convenience store section and an Internet section. Each area has its own different lighting – food service is warm and golden and frozen food is flourescent.

Offerings are not the usual run of the mill, lower priced, mass merchandise. Gone are the Twinkies, Slurpees and fried chicken under heat lamps in favor of croissants, local specialities (foie gras in Paris), cappuchino and herbal teas. Stores bake their own breads and pastries and make gourmet soups and sandwiches to the customer's order.

Finally, consumers can logon at E-kiosks to browse the Internet (at a nominal charge) or use an integrated video camera to take and send videos of themselves (from a gas pump/station?). To pay for this, customers can buy prepaid cards that enable them to use their minutes any time they want.

All of this is part of BP's attempt to rebrand itself as environmentally friendly. In that scenario BP doesn't stand for British Petroleum, it stands for Beyond Petroleum. The recently re-designed sunburst logo is part of this environmental approach. To protect customers at the pump from the elements, BP uses a canopy that contains thin-film solar technology that will generate electricity to run the pumps. The sunburst reinforces the idea of solar energy.

As with any branding effort, BP needs to support the new stations with advertising. In the latter half of the year 2000, they introduced new ads that focused on BP's role as a green company. Using print and television ads, they posed the questions: "Is it possible to drive a car and still have a clean environment? Can business go further and be a force for good?"

To be successful, BP will have to increase credibility for its environmental claims. Consumers in England criticized the Beyond Petroleum move and suggested that Big Polluter would be more accurate. To gain credibility, BP might have to spend millions of pounds investing in solar energy through ventures such as solar-powered factories that produce BP products.

Even ignoring issues of credibility, one has to wonder if consumers are really interested in going back into the station. Some critics scoff at all of these efforts and ask do you want to buy your food where you buy gasoline? Does the smell of gasoline go with gourmet sandwiches? Does it make sense to re-train consumers to spend more time at the gas station after spending the 1990s speeding their trip through the station? Is there any evidence that consumers want all these coupons and foodstuffs and e-information at the pump? Finally, this author wants to know if you want to be the person waiting for the customer ahead of you to look up directions on the e-screen at the pump?

Discussion Questions

1. What needs of consumers are the gasoline retailers attempting to meet?
2. What types of purchase decisions is BP attempting to stimulate?
3. Which of these efforts are likely to be successful, if any? Why? Why will the others not be successful?
4. Are there situations in which each of these strategies could be successful?
5. Attitudes consist of knowledge, feelings and behavior. How is the BP Connect strategy attempting to affect each of these components of attitudes?

References

-----, "Bizmodel.com," <u>Informationweek</u>, January 29, 2001, p. 126.

-----, "A real gasser," <u>Progressive Grocer</u>, March 2001, p. 10.

Andrew-Jones, Gareth and Annie Moreton, "Will consumers give 'green' BP a chance?" <u>Marketing</u>, August 17, 2000, p. 7.

Bauroth, Nan, "Edgewater and Marconi, Priming the New-Economy Pump," <u>Bizlife North Carolina</u>, March 2001, pp. 17ff.

Cassy, John, "BP brings power of the sun to pumps," <u>The Guardian</u>, December 12, 200, p. 28.

Jenkins, Zamora, "Fill 'er up? <u>The Oil and Gas Journal</u>, December 18, 2000, p. 17.

Trivedi, Kruti, "BP Amoco wants to sell much more than gas at tits new stations," <u>The New York Times</u>, July 25, 200, p. C6.

Princess for a Day

He popped the question and she said, "Yes." Now begins the planning for one of the most elaborate rituals in the U.S. – a wedding. Those who are inexperienced cannot begin to appreciate what is about to happen. From selecting a dress, finding a date when the church or wedding site is available, deciding on receptions, food, music, bridesmaids, endless showers, lunches, to place cards for the guests and the bows on the flower girl's hat, this is a multi-month – frequently a year-long – process. Couples routinely seem to expect six-month engagements, nowadays.

Over 2.4 million couples tied the knot in the year 2000. To do so, they spent over $32 billion dollars with the average wedding costing over $20,000 in the U.S. And the honeymoon will only add to the cost. Who is going to pay for this? The answer to that question fifty years ago or even thirty years ago might have been "parents," but today's couple is older and more financially secure. In the last forty years, the average age for men getting married for the first time has risen from 25.2 to 29.5; for women it has increased from 22.5 to 27.4. These older couples are more likely to be college graduates and they have worked for several years. As they take on more of the expense themselves, they are able to suggest that interfering parents back off. Paying their own way gives them more control over the details of the wedding and the opportunity to do what they *want* rather than what parents think *appropriate*.

Given the elaborate nature of wedding planning, where does the bride-to-be start? It's either the dress, the date and site, or the food for the wedding. The order of these three items might vary, with perhaps the date coming first because of the need to make reservations. Then there may be an interaction between the site and the food (what can be served where). Dates and sites are a matter of what's available around the time that the couple hopes to get married; whereas food is not so much a matter of the actual menu as the type of food – a full meal or just finger foods. Once the date, site and type of food are settled, the bride's attention focuses on selecting the right dress.

To start this process, she has stored memories and dreams from weddings that she has already attended and sessions at sleepovers in which she and her friends giggled, oohed and aahed over bridal magazines when they were growing up. Nowadays, these same brides-in-waiting can buy InStyle Weddings and pore over celebrity weddings. Catherine Zeta Jones and Michael Douglas probably had the most publicized wedding since Princess Di wed Prince Charles (available on videotape). By being willing to sell the rights to photos and "the story of their love and wedding." Catherine and Michael were able to recoup the cost of their more than $1,000,000 wedding.

As if that weren't enough, the young woman and her friends can watch the Wedding Channel – a television show that describes the planning of real weddings. Some young women even admit to watching the show with their boyfriends. (Now, that's throwing the guy a hint.)

But this treasury of stored memories, images and dreams are hard to convert to reality, so brides must turn to "real" information sources. Which ones can or do they use? Recent studies show that 24% of engaged women use the Internet as their *primary* source of information for planning their wedding and a total of 62% do some of their wedding shopping on the Internet. What sorts of web sites do they use? There are two major ones – WeddingChannel.com and TheKnot.com.

When this researcher investigated the WeddingChannel.com, it was obvious that wedding planning and bridal registries were the major items prospective couples were looking for. Under planning, gowns were mentioned first. To get an idea of prices, I asked for gowns of any type by any designer that were over $5,000 and 40 dresses were promptly shown on the screen. In the $2,000 to 5,000 range, there were another 200; in the $500 to $2,000 range, there was another 200; in the $200 to $500 range, there were 70 and below $200, there were only two. Thus, 39.1% of the dresses shown were in the $2,000 to $5,000 range and 78.1% of the dresses were in the $500 to $5,000 range. There were considerably more very high end dresses (over $5,000) than there were low-end dresses (under $200). Unwilling to register at another bridal registry (which would mean lying about my identity, age, marital status and being bombarded with hundreds of email wedding ads to go with all the low-rate mortgage and credit offers I already receive via email), I was not able to search TheKnot. However, they claimed to have over 20,000 gowns in their listings in five price ranges (very affordable, affordable, moderately expensive, expensive and very expensive). Expensive seems to account for more of the price ranges and probably more of the dresses.

If you are willing to register at all these sites, the Internet makes comparison shopping easy and provides an incredible variety of dresses, cake styles and flower styles and thousands of wedding tips. This enables the bride to gather a lot of information before she ever sets foot in a bridal salon.

In addition to the Internet, there are magazines that provide information to the bride-to-be. The long-time favorites are *Brides* and *Modern Bride*. Both are fat magazines with what seems like more than 90% advertisements. The average circulation of *Brides* in 2000 was 420,000 and the average page count was 850 pages. For *Modern Bride*, the average circulation was 400,000 and the average page count was 800 pages. Besides those two magazines (weighed in pounds), there's *Bridal Guide* (circulation of about 265,000 and 400 pages) and *Elegant Bride* (circulation of 150,000 and 250 pages). Those four magazines accounted for the vast majority of magazine sales until Martha Stewart entered the market with her publication Martha Stewart *Weddings* which was estimated to have grabbed a circulation of 375,000 with about 400 pages in less than a year.

Traditionally, bridal magazines have featured page after page of wedding dresses, and although Martha Stewart's publication is entitled *Weddings*, it's no exception. Although Martha started with a smaller book (as magazines are called), it's getting larger with each addition. All magazines feature planning tips and have articles on cakes, flowers, receptions, bridesmaid gifts and dresses, etc., but Martha Stewart seems to have more ideas for the wedding. Focus group research revealed that nearly all participants (over 50 in total) thought that Martha Stewart would have more ideas. This perception was based on anticipations, not actual experience with the magazine. This means that the image of her magazine is based on other experiences with and knowledge of Martha Stewart. Because she is known for having lots and lots of decorating ideas, readers expect the same to be true of her bridal magazine.

When we think about the positioning of bridal magazines, it becomes clear that publishers have traditionally positioned their magazines to appeal to the first part of the decision process – the dress; whereas Martha Stewart appeared to position her magazine for the wedding planning process rather than selection of the dress. With each successive issue, however, her magazines are getting bigger and they have more dresses in them. Will this change the perception of the magazine?

What other sources of information are available to the bride-to-be? There's word-of-mouth among friends. Discussing weddings is something that many young women want to do. In these sessions, well-thumbed copies of magazines are passed around and evaluations are shared. Weddings of older siblings and then weddings of friends are dissected remorselessly so that young women come to have strongly-held ideas about the wedding that they want before they are even engaged.

While magazines and the Internet can provide a lot of information, no woman is willing to buy a wedding dress without actually feeling the fabric, trying on dresses and closely examining the results. Thus, bridal salons become extremely important. In this cocooned world, the bride-to-be is waited on attentively by sales staff, mothers and friends. The virtues of many dresses may be discussed at length and measurements taken to make the dress fit perfectly. This cosseting experience is the appropriate setting for selecting the wedding dress, which many refer to as *the princess dress*. Selecting the right dress cannot be done without reinforcement from others. The audience has to agree that this is the right princess dress for this bride.

Given high divorce rates, one might think that the importance of weddings would decline, but a look at the generation getting married reveals that that is not so. Most of today's brides are "Generation Xers". They were born between 1965 and 1976. Generation Xers are part of the "I" generation who have been labeled rebels and influencers. They were latchkey children who entertained themselves after school when their parents or more likely (single) parent came home from work. In addition to divorce, this generation witnessed a series of social disappointments such as the Challenger space shuttle explosion in 1986 and the growth and maturity of the AIDS virus. As a consequence, many of these bridal consumers are determined to do better; they are committed to making their marriage a lasting success. They are entrepreneurial, highly educated, very technologically advanced, expect to take charge of their future and are very likely to voice their concerns, and opinions and wedding planning is no exception..

Younger brides (born after 1976) are members of Generation Y which is the "all" generation. They grew up in an age of optimism, recycling, knowing how to live in the present to take care of the future and brand loyalty. They respond to messages that acknowledge their intelligence, share new ideas, are community-oriented and inspire health. They are also very computer literate and process information in a multi-tasking manner.

One might expect very rational decision-making from these groups when they enter the bridal salon, but something else seems to happen. The recognition that this is the bride's day starts to permeate decision-making so that little expense or effort is spared in creating the "perfect" wedding. At this point, what they *want* matters more than what they can *afford* or what makes "sense". Couple that with an ability and willingness to pick up the tab if parents are either unwilling or unable, and one has a recipe for an explosion of wedding spending.

To understand this better, let's listen to four young women (late twenties) describe their attitudes toward wedding dresses.

> Alice: "When I was growing up, we lived in northern Jersey and often
> shopped in New York. Once when I was ten – I think I was ten or about
> that – we were in Saks and happened to walk past a bridal display. I saw
> the *most gorgeous* dress and I knew right then that I would buy my dress
> in Saks. I have always believed that."

Did she? Even though she now lives in the Southeast? Yep, first thing after getting that diamond, she and Mom flew to New York and shopped for nearly a week. Where did they find a dress? Saks of course! It had to be ordered and altered, so she won't even get it for months, but it's the right dress – she knows that in her heart. And she and her friends have discussed it any number of times – they can't wait to see it.

One of Alice's friends who is already married and had had to hold the line on the cost of her dress actually bought hers in a chain of discount bridal salons. According to Vicky:

> "I knew I couldn't spend a lot on a dress. After all, my budget was only
> $15,000. So, I shopped at (name of chain) and out of all the dresses there,
> I could easily tell which one was right for me. It was satiny and simple
> with a high waist and was embroidered down the front. It really stood out
> from the other dresses, because they were all covered in lace. There's lace
> everywhere – on the bodice and sleeves…and they were all white – really
> white-white – no cream or ivory."

At this point, Alice chimes in

> "I looked in those places too, not just at Saks. Yeah, the dresses are all
> lace and have puffy sleeves..and trains. They are too white and so-o-o-o
> eighties."

Alice and Vicky's two friends, one of whom is engaged, chime in. "It's true. They're all lace and puffy sleeved. They are just too cute – not elegant at all and you want your dress to be elegant."

When asked what constitutes an elegant dress, they look at you as if you are stone stupid not to know…"Why, they're classy, simple, have clean lines and wonderful fabrics. They make you look like what-was-her name? The blonde who married the prince? Oh, yeah, Kelly, Grace Kelly! That's who you want to look like. She would never wear something that was fussy and covered in lace – especially that stiff, cheap lace," says Kelly, Alice's friend.

When asked why they think salons carry dresses like that (lacy and puffy-sleeved), the four women are silent for a few moments and finally, tentatively suggest that well, there are a lot of people who like that kind of thing. And, they point out, that after all, we *are* discussing discount chains.

What is so amazing is the similarity of taste that these four women (all in their late twenties and all doing well in their chosen careers) exhibit. They are all agreed on the appropriate style of dress. They all know about sources of information about dresses – they could name internet sites right away—and can discuss bridal magazines without needing to look at any actual magazines. If Vicky had not had a budget constraint, she would no doubt have flown off to New York as well, but she is not embarrassed about buying her dress at the discount salon.

What magazines do they like? They really prefer *Elegant Bride*. They comment that *Brides* and *Modern Bride* are just page after page of advertisements. When asked if the advertisements are useful in selecting a dress, they ask "Where are you going to buy the dress after you see the ad?" Even Alice (our New York shopper) says, "I looked at those magazines and I couldn't find those dresses in stores!" What do they think of Martha Stewart? They actually seem to wilt over the idea of Martha Stewart and point out that she's good for lots of ideas, but who wants to make their own place cards or tie the bows on the chairs at the reception. As one of them commented, "you might get some ideas there (in Martha's magazine), but you have too many other things to do to actually make all those things for yourself." They all groan just thinking about it.

Those four women are Gen Xers. What would we hear if we listened to a group of Generation Y? A focus group of undergraduate students had very different ideas. They, too, had looked at all the magazines, but because they weren't engaged yet, they really hadn't checked out the Internet. That did not mean that they didn't have strong ideas about dresses. Their preferences were for strapless dresses or dresses with spaghetti straps, form-fitting and low cut – front and back. When discussing dresses, they were all agreeing with this idea of the perfect wedding dress until one of them said "Well, that's what I want, but I probably won't get it." "Why not?" the others asked. "Well," she said, "my grandmother will be there. I couldn't get married without my grandmother, and she would be horrified if I wore a low-cut gown." This caused the others to pause and deliberate for a few moments before agreeing that that would probably be true for them as well until one of them broke in with "Really, I'm a lot less worried about my grandmother than I am my father! He would skin me alive if I walked down the aisle showing too much cleavage!" This produced a lot of laughter and agreement from the others who said things like, "Yeah, my dad would be like that too. He would never let his 'little girl' reveal too much." However, the group seemed reluctant to dismiss the low cut gowns and one girl wistfully said "Well, probably by the time I have a daughter getting married, ideas will change and she can wear my low cut gown – the one I didn't get to wear!" When asked about the lacy dresses, they also look at you like you're stupid – another group that doesn't want that lace.

Their attitudes on magazines diverge from their older sisters, however. They liked *Brides* and *Modern Bride* magazines because these books were so fat that the women assumed that they must have lots of good information. Did the fact that most of the dresses pictured therein were in ads bother them? No. They just wanted to see lots of dresses.

And they had strong ideas about the models on the covers. They preferred models who appeared to be in their mid-twenties and who were relatively serious about this. If the model was standing one-sided, this seemed to connote that she wasn't taking this seriously. Also, she couldn't be laughing – again that wasn't serious. There was a strong relationship between hairstyles and dresses. Long hair should be worn up with regular dresses and down with those strapless dresses. They didn't think brides should wear much jewelry and they didn't like tiaras. They preferred veils. Overall, they seemed to favor models with a somewhat sophisticated, but almost simple appearance – not too much makeup, fussy hair styles (bits of hair dangling everywhere was a no-no) and relatively little jewelry.

When asked about where they would like to have their weddings, there was a sharp division within the women. One group – about 60% of each group – said that they would get married in a church. The primary reason was religion. Several women who were Roman Catholic said that they really didn't have any other option, but most of the protestants agreed that they preferred to be married in a church as that seemed to be more fitting – after all, it is a religious ceremony as well as a civil one they said.

What was of more interest was where the reception would be held. Indeed, the reception seemed to be of more importance to most of them than the wedding. Wedding ceremonies are remarkably similar across churches, but receptions are not. Almost none of the women wanted to have their reception in the church hall – that was very definitely *out*. Instead they wanted to have the reception at more upscale meeting places such as country clubs, local mansions, bed and breakfasts and elegant hotels – even some private dining facilities.

The importance of the reception was apparent in their attitude that one must show guests a good time. The site of the reception, the food and the music set the tone for remembrances of the wedding because the reception actually takes longer. The group of women in the Gen X group remembered Vicky's reception in detail and talked about how great it was. Vicky commented, "I would have been embarrassed if I couldn't have shown the guests a good time. These are my friends from college and childhood. Some of them came all across the United States to the wedding. The family I lived with in Germany (as a high school exchange student) also came to the wedding. They spent a lot of money. How could I have had a stand-up affair with finger food?"

Her friend Kelly agreed by saying "I'm from Connecticut and Robbie's from Georgia. Where are we getting married? Here (Middle Atlantic), which is sort of half-way for everyone. We aren't inviting them to come all that distance for chicken wings! In Connecticut where I grew up, there was a mansion outside town that would have been perfect for a wedding. It was sort of an Italian villa with large terraces overlooking the ocean. Just think if you had an evening reception with dance music and lights strung around the terrace what a romantic setting…" The other women dreamily agreed.

The younger women had fewer details in mind, but they also expressed an interest in having a big reception and showing guests a good time. They were especially interested in music and hiring the right kind of band (one that could play a wide range of music to suit different guests' tastes) was extremely important. For both groups, dancing seemed to be an expression of enjoyment on the part of the guests. Somewhere in this discussion, one woman said "And let's face it. We have to have a bar. Without alcohol, no one will dance!" No dancing seems to be the seal of doom on a reception. Having guests standing around making chitchat would be most upsetting to these women.

After the wedding and reception, there was actually very little discussion of the honeymoon. It seemed to pale in comparison with the wedding itself.

A few days later, this researcher was having lunch with a friend whose three daughters are between 23 and 30. She has been to a lot of weddings recently – a lot of weddings! When I told her about the research, she said, "That's like my experience. They all want these expensive affairs that go on for hours afterward. The idea of weddings as a celebration has thoroughly permeated this age group. They really want to get all their 'loved ones' together and celebrate the marriage. But you know…there's a sameness about all of these weddings. I can predict what they're going to be like – lots of food, same music/same dancing, expensive dress and while they all have a theme, once you get beneath the theme (outdoors, romantic, Italian, whatever) they're very much the same. Lots of people, sit-down dinners, dancing, smart and witty toasts and fashionable guests. I don't know that they've achieved much individuality beyond the theme." Hm-m-m-m, so much for all this wedding planning.

Some of the most startling statistics about U.S. society concern marriage. Nearly 50% of those $20,000+ weddings ends in divorce. Only 64% of people getting married in the U.S. are getting married for the first time. This means that 36% are getting married for the second, third, fourth, fifth, who knows how many times? Census data from the year 2000 indicate that the percentage of married couple households declined from 55% in 1990 to 52%. The percentage of female-headed households with children in the home increased by 25% in the same period. But that is only part of the picture. The number of unmarried-partner-homes (couples living together) increased from 3 to 5% of the population. These couples cite personal beliefs and the so-called marriage penalty on federal income tax as deterrents to being married. One respondent says "We've talked about it several times and could get hitched in a heartbeat, but we haven't seen a need for it."

Those firms involved in the bridal industry need not cringe, however. The echo boomers (teens and pre-teens) or children of the baby boomers constitute the second biggest population bulge ever in the U.S. They are the mirror for the baby boomers in terms of size and willingness to spend – after all they grew up in homes headed by the boomers who in the eighties were into more, more, more and quality in everything. If bridal trends continue, this could be a very free-spending group.

And if it doesn't work out, does it matter? "No," according to one recent divorcee. "The marriage ended but I still have an investment in the dress. I saved it to keep the happiness of that time alive for my son. It is a piece of my history."

It appears that the wedding ritual has meaning whether the marriage has a storybook ending or not. Could we stretch that to suggest that the ritual is more important than living happily ever after? That's it's better to have wed than never to have?

Remember there were four women discussing Vicky and Alice's wedding, but we never heard from the fourth one, Sally, who isn't engaged and has no prospects on the horizon. At one point, she looked thoroughly miserable and almost began crying while staring at the table. "I don't know what I'll do. At the rate I'm going, I may never get married, " she whispered. "Don't worry," the others told her. "Your day will come." Unfortunately, she really seems to need that reinforcement.

Questions for Discussion

1. Describe the information search process that young women go through for planning weddings? How does this match with the information search process described in your textbook?
2. What is the role that each information source plays? Why is each important?
3. What kind of decision-making does this case describe?
4. What are the important group and family effects on the wedding dress decision process? What function(s) does each group/family factor perform?
5. What kind of ritual is a wedding? What does it symbolize?
6. What's the importance/symbolism of *princess for a day*?
7. Is a wedding sacred or profane consumption?
8. Were the descriptions of the Gen Xers and Gen Yers focus group comments consistent with the image of these groups as subcultures?
9. How can the concept of social class be used to explain the focus group results and the discussion of what dresses were sold at the discount bridal salon?
10. If you were a wedding counselor, how could you use the information in this case to customize plans for a couple?
11. What does the case illustrate about segmentation of the bridal industry?
12. If you owned stores that sold wedding dresses and accessories, how could you use the information in the case?

References

Armas, Genaro, "Family makeup changed vastly in last decade," Greensboro News and Record, May 15, 2001, p. A1 & A5.

"Bride' s," HFN The Weekly Newspaper for the Home Furnishing Network, Nov. 18, 1996, v. 70, n. 47, p. 34.

"Bridal magazines 'gloriously strong,'" Advertising Age, April 18, 1988, v. 59, n. 17, p. S22(3).

Bridal magazines open new front in war for ad dollars: 'Modern Bride' takes early lead in pages for '97," Advertising Age, June 16, 1997, v. 68, n. 24, p. 3 (2).

Fried, Lisa, "Battle at the altar," Folio: the Magazine for Magazine Management, June 1, 19991, v. 20, n. 6, p. 31 (4).

"Martha Stewart Omnimedia plans internal expansion," Home Textiles Today, June 26, 2000, v. 21, issue 42, p. 29.

McDowell, Jeanne, "Martha Stewart," <u>Working Woman</u>, June 200, v. 25, issue 6, p. 60

Nelson, Luann, "Dashing down the bridal path," <u>Business North Carolina</u>, June 1991, v. 11, n. 6, p. 68 (6).

"Weddings: a $35 billion market," <u>Target Marketing</u>, May 1998, v. 21, n. 5, p. 66 (3).

St. Timothy's: Struggling to Survive

Prologue

Stan Simpson – normally pastor of the new St. Timothy's United Methodist Church, but currently painter of kitchen baseboards – jumped as a loud crash in his vicinity echoed through the house. Looking through his paint spattered glasses, Stan saw Jeff, one of the original members of the new church, looking sheepishly at the tray of white paint he had just knocked off the ladder. Carol, Jeff's wife, was simultaneously staring at the spilled paint and trying not to laugh. "Jeff is just as clumsy here as he is at home" she thought. When she could restrain her laughter no longer, both Stan and Jeff joined in.

Things were going well, Stan thought. The house, located on the property where the future church would be built, was nearly refurbished and would serve well as a meeting place for small groups and socials, choir practice room, and church office until a new church building could be constructed. Architectural plans, a construction date and budget had not been set for the new facility. Stan knew that the dedication and perseverance shown by everyone involved in repairing and updating their current facility proved that they believed in the undertaking.

As Stan watched Carol and Jeff clean up the paint, he was a little uneasy. Just that afternoon, he had gotten a research report based on a survey conducted in church two weeks before. The results of that and the fluctuations in attendance had him worried. He felt that the church needed to attract more members and very regular church-going members at that. But it was proving more difficult than he had thought to appeal to the diverse community that his church served.

The Church's Goal and Problem

Stan Simpson is the pastor of the recently founded St. Timothy's United Methodist Church in the Willard's Boundary development in a Midwestern city. His church was a spin-off of a well established church, Christ United Methodist Church, in the heart of the city. To get St. Timothy's off the ground, the local District Association of the United Methodist Church and Christ United had underwritten a three-year budget for the fledgling church. Eventually, however, pledges from members would have to replace those funds in supporting the church's program. Getting pledges meant getting members and he only had a little over two years left!

In the initial three-year period, Stan had to "plan" the new church in terms of its character, mode of operation, find a suitable site and begin operations. In the interim period, St. Timothy's would need to reach and maintain a critical mass of 80 to 120 weekly worshippers who contributed a minimum of $1,000 just to receive support from the Conference. To be considered successful, St. Timothy's would need 125 to 175 regular worshippers by the end of the three-year period in order to justify construction of a church building. If they failed to meet that attendance goal…well…no one wanted to think about that. Stan had started St. Timothy's confidant that they could begin construction in three years. Now, he was not as sure.

So far, Stan and his followers had spent nearly a year planning for the new church and beginning worship services. St. Timothy's held its first service on December 4 with 150 worshippers; but since then, attendance had fluctuated from a low of 43 to a high of 132. In the last two months, attendance hovered in the 90 to 105 range. St. Timothy's attendance figures since inception are shown in Table 1. Average attendance was 87 individuals. Given the fluctuation in attendance, it was hard to say how many regular worshippers there were at St. Timothy's but clearly the church had not met either the critical mass or the success goal.

St. Timothy's Location

St. Timothy's United Methodist Church served the fast growing western side of a small Midwestern city with a population of 250,000. Twenty years ago, few people had lived in the five-mile strip between the city's west side and a local community named Parkersburg. With the exception of an upscale housing area called Ridgefield, most of the housing in that strip was relatively modest and dispersed between trailer parks, retailers (Chuck's Auto Painting and Garage) and businesses such as veterinarians.

By the early 1990s, however, the city was rapidly expanding westward. This expansion encouraged a consortium of builders to purchase a large tract in the county, which they developed into a community of over 1,000 homes called Willard's Boundary. Most of these were single family dwellings with a few townhouse units and two large apartment complexes. Housing prices ranged from the low $120,000s to over $250,000. As a result, the area attracted mostly upper-middle class households with a variety of ethnic backgrounds and family composition. The success of Willard's Boundary sparked other developers to plan smaller developments of higher priced housing in adjoining areas. Thus, this semi-rural area changed dramatically in a few years as the population mushroomed from a few thousand to more than 12,000 individuals.

The church purchased a ranch house on a two-acre lot adjacent to the Willard's Boundary development. This building contained the offices of the pastor and the part-time Assistant Director of Communications, storage space and choir practice facilities. In addition, small groups frequently met in the former living room of the house and, in good weather, larger groups met on the lawn. Because the house was hidden behind a stand of trees, there was a large sign next to the driveway informing passersby of the church's existence. Unfortunately, the house was not large enough for Sunday worship, which was held in the auditorium of the community college in Parkersburg several miles away.

The Decision to Found a New Church

Two factors led to the found of St. Timothy's. The first was a need for growth in the United Methodist Church and the other was the desire of Stan Simpson who was associate pastor at Christ United Methodist Church, a large traditional church in the city, to found a church.

According to the United Methodist News Service, the United Methodist denomination was, as a whole, growing older than the U.S. population at large. Over sixty percent of the Methodist laity was 50 years or older. To be viable in the future, the denomination needed to attract younger congregants. A study conducted by the state conference of the United Methodist Conference indicated that the Willard's Boundary area was under-churched. When combined with the recognition that Willard's Boundary was composed primarily of young families, this finding led to what seemed like an obvious choice – the decision to locate a new church in or near Willard's Boundary.

Given the rapid growth of Willard's Boundary and the fact that the Methodists had not started a new church in the city in 35 years, it is easy to understand why the Methodist Conference was excited about starting a new church there, but to understand the motivations of Stan Simpson, it is necessary to examine his background.

Stan Simpson grew up in Kentucky and attended Western Kentucky College – after which he obtained a Master of Divinity degree from Duke University. Upon graduation, he served as pastor in a small town in West Virginia before going back to school at the University of Virginia where he obtained a Master of Arts in Ethics. Then, he spent three years at a church in Kentucky before moving to Christ United Methodist Church where he served as an assistant minister. While there, he began a doctorate at Princeton University.

Christ United Methodist is a large church – 1900 members – even though it is relatively young – only thirty-seven years old. In addition to Stan, the church employed a senior minister and another assistant minister. It has a traditional church hierarchy and is an established influence in the community. Although he enjoyed service at Christ United Methodist, Stan realized that when his appointment there ended, he would not be old enough or experienced enough to become the head pastor at such a large church. Knowing that he would have to make a move, Stan thought very seriously about what kind of move he wanted to make. Finally, he decided that he would like to lead the establishment of a new church – one that catered more to the changing cultural and demographic face of America. He realized that many of the U.S. population either because of racial, ethnic or demographic background felt uncomfortable and even lost in large, traditional churches. To him, Willard's Boundary with its diverse population was a community in great need of a new church and he wanted to be the pastor of that church. A church with such a diverse population would need an atypical minister and Stan's background qualified him for that position!

But Stan could not do this alone. Seventeen members of Christ United Methodist volunteered to help Stan found the church. Why? One reason was location as nearly half of them lived in the Willard's Boundary area. Ken believed that the others were "pioneers" – people who liked to start things, who thrived on the excitement and stimulation of something new, who wanted to develop their own kind of church and who wanted a challenge. According to Larry Melton, one of the "pioneers", the group migrated to St. Timothy's because they believed in Stan Simpson's spiritual leadership and charisma.

Planning the New Church

Once they obtained the backing of the Conference and Christ United Methodist Church, Stan and his pioneers began meeting to plan their new church. The fist issues they tackled were the name of the church and the church's mission statement. They chose the name, St. Timothy's based on three references from the Second Book of Paul to Timothy. In II Timothy 1.5, Paul discusses the faith existing in several previous generations of Timothy's family. As Timothy's grandmother and mother passed their faith on to Timothy, so Christ United Methodist Church was passing its faith on to the new church. Also, in II Timothy 1.6, Paul called for a spiritual renewal. The new church represented a renewal of the spirit that kindled Christ United Methodist Church. Finally, II Timothy 1.7 called for a boldness of spirit to testify for the church. Thus, the new name looked back to the church's heritage but also led strongly and purposefully toward a new life in the spirit.

Small groups met to formulate the church's mission statement. They discussed the characteristics of the kind of church they wanted to build, the kind of church they thought that God wanted and the kind of church that would that would best serve the needs of the area. Their final output was a set of eleven characteristics that the group thought defined the vision/mission of St. Timothy's. (See Table 2.) St. Timothy's chose to position itself as a pluralistic congregation believing in individual spirituality, openness, and respect for diversity.

The pioneer group also visited six other new churches in the area to obtain insights on how to start their new church. These visits emphasized: (1) the importance of getting small groups together for fun and fellowship to build a feeling of community; (2) the use of friendly, non-threatening visits by lay people to first-time visitors; (3) the importance of having new members establish a financial giving program to generate a sense of belonging; and most importantly (4) the importance of spirituality – an awareness of and dedication to a task ordained and sustained by God. They also formed study groups on subjects such as "Coping as Christians" and "Faith Seeking Understanding" and training for the Stephen Ministry – volunteers who meet for an hour a week with individuals suffering some crisis, transition or grief.

While planning was underway, the new church bought the two acre-site and began refurbishing the house. Every weekend for several months, volunteers worked at the site, stripping walls and carpets, cleaning, painting, putting down new flooring and mowing the lawn. In October, they were able to move in office equipment so that Stan and his "staff" could work from their "new" offices.

Contacting the Potential Congregation

By October, the pioneers were in a position to begin outreach efforts promoting the church. They realized that the church should attract members from the many individuals in the area who did not attend church rather than stealing members of other churches. According to a 1988 Gallup Poll, 44% of American Adults are "unchurched," meaning that they do not belong to a church or have not attended church services, other than holidays, weddings or funerals, in six months. Over 72% of these unchurched adults, however, reported that they pray regularly and 58% said they were open to join a church if they found the right one. This data suggested that a substantial target market might exist from which to build St. Timothy's congregation.

In a two-week period, church volunteers began identifying prospects. Using a telephone bank at the community college, they contacted 3,000 homes in the three zip codes surrounding the new church's location. When they identified an individual not participating in a local church, callers asked if the respondent would like to receive information concerning a new church being formed in the community. For those answering "yes," the individual's address was recorded on the church's mailing list. The telephone calls produced a list of 378 households that were interested in receiving mailings about St. Timothy's. When combined with names gathered through earlier research, the church compiled a mailing list of nearly 700 households.

At the same time, Stan contacted other churches in the area to determine the size of their membership and the types of outreach efforts they used to contact potential members. Table 3 shows the results of this investigation.

As part of his area study, Stan also characterized the local churches as conservative, traditional or liberal. Conservative churches were those with highly authoritarian pastoral leadership, a strong hierarchy in the church, a tendency to be conservative politically and to have more strict interpretations of scripture. Liberal churches were less likely to equate conservative and social values to being a Christian. Their congregations tended to include more individuals in second marriages with blended families. Traditional churches fell in the middle of the spectrum. While they are not as authoritarian as conservative churches, they do lean toward traditional worship practices.

St. Timothy's would be classified as pluralistic because of its diverse nature. While the church would draw on tradition, it would also incorporate non-dogmatic elements. Such a positioning, Stan thought, would appeal to the church's target market. Although Willard's Boundary was relatively homogeneous in terms of income – upper middle class and above – it is diverse in terms of racial and ethnic composition as many Asian Americans lived in the area. In addition, there are many second marriage households and divorcees. Surrounding Willard's Boundary is a wider range of income groups from the well-heeled in Ridgefield to lower income households in the trailer parks. Stan believed that St. Timothy's positioning efforts have been successful because he has observed some members of all of these groups attending services at St. Timothy's.

Marketing studies of church outreach and promotional efforts, like Stan's, are the subject of a hot debate in the religious establishment. On one hand, many traditional religious leaders felt that aggressive marketing efforts belittled the spirit of Christianity by over-emphasizing big attendance. On the other hand, some religious experts, like statistician George Barna, espoused the virtues of "seeker-sensitive" churches, or those who openly marketed to expand attendance. In Barna's opinion, each time a church prints bulletins or develops signage, that church is marketing, and he believes churches can focus on a key community group without prostituting religious values, theology or purposes. Because he was well aware of tension created by church marketing, Stan Simpson realized that outreach efforts at St. Timothy's would need to walk a fine line.

Two and a half months before their first service, St. Timothy's sent a series of mailings to potential members. The first mailing contained the vision statement and was sent to all 12,000 residents in the three zip codes in the church's immediate area. The church targeted subsequent mailings to interested respondents from the telephone survey. The messages in the first three of these mailings concerned children, adults and the vision of the church. The last was an invitation to the first service on December 4. In addition, the church bought a mailing list of seven hundred households that were not regular church members and sent them mailings. Finally, members of the church stuffed mailboxes in Willard's Boundary during the fall.

Building Interest In the Church

To make the church more attractive to new members, St. Timothy's sponsored a number of group activities designed specifically for members to meet and become acquainted with each other. Church members started small rotating dinner groups and a middle school-age fellowship group along with the traditional adult leadership group, a continuing bible study group and several other study groups. Members of one group, Vines and Branches, studied the life of Christ. A men's group studied the book *Promise Keepers*, which focuses on men and their relationship with God, their roles as husbands and fathers, and their responsibilities in the workplace. The women had a retreat to define their role in the new church. There were special holiday observances including a communion, plays at Christmas and an Eggstravaganza at Easter. Other volunteers worked on the Habitat House, an effort that provides the labor to build a house for lower-income families.

St. Timothy's also focused on getting to know and be known by individuals in the community. To provide personal contact, members visited first-time guests on the Monday following their attendance at a worship service. The weekly newsletter, *Seven Days*, distributed to members and others on the mailing list, contained news about members, activities of the congregation, and inspirational messages. These, as well as the group activities mentioned above, created closer contact between members and guests and enhanced their feeling of belonging in the church community.

Stan observed that many individuals don't worship because they feel lost in larger, more established churches. Divorcees and members of blended families especially may not feel comfortable in those settings. Therefore, he actively promoted opportunities for individuals to engage in small group activities where they would not feel overwhelmed and would feel more at ease. As a result, these activities should build a spirit of friendliness and relationships which are the characteristics most heavily sought by unchurched adults according to <u>Christianity Today</u>.

Services at St. Timothy's signaled the different atmosphere of the church. Stan wore a white robe, rather than the traditional black one and there was no recitation or reading aloud by the congregation during the service. In addition, participants need not "dress up" to attend. Church members hoped that the low key, more casual atmosphere would be appealing to individuals uncomfortable with the more traditional church service.

The Marketing Research Project

In February, Stan talked to a professor at the community college about doing some marketing research for the church. Three students volunteered for the project and met with Stan several times before developing the questionnaire shown in Exhibit 3. They pre-tested the questionnaire in an adult study group session and distributed it at a Sunday worship service in March.

Originally the students had hoped to obtain eighty complete questionnaires. On the Sunday of the survey, there were 95 individuals, including children, in the congregation, which resulted in the collection of 46 complete questionnaires as there could only be one completed for each household.

Table 3 summarizes the results of the survey. Fellowship and overall spirituality were the primary motivators for attending church. Respondents ranked the worship service and pastor's skills as the most important aspects of church services. Similarly, the majority were very satisfied with the worship service and pastor's skills at St. Timothy's. Youth programs and music were less important.

Later That Evening

Distracted by his musings about the church's attendance issues and the results of the survey, Stan was startled when Jeff and Carol called out "We're leaving now." Recovering quickly, Stan called out "Will you be here for the meeting tomorrow night?" and Jeff responded "Sure. See you then."

As he listened to their car drive away, Stan's thoughts wandered back to the survey. Stan was a little surprised that youth and adult programs were not very important to respondents since he and the "pioneers" had put so much effort into those programs. He was also perturbed that the youth programs had not gotten better ratings. Thinking along those lines caused him to wish that they had asked more demographic questions. The students had originally suggested that, but Stan had vetoed it because he thought that asking for race or ethnicity might put some respondents on the spot because their questionnaires would be easily identifiable.

The more he thought about it, the more he thought that maybe they should have asked more penetrating questions about what people wanted from a church and what was important to them. "Ah, well, too late for that now," he thought.

Elsewhere In WIllard's Boundary: Stories of Potential Congregants

Stan is right that he might have gotten better results if the research team had probed more deeply into the backgrounds and motivations of his church members. But that would only be part of the story. What might be more important for him to learn would be more about potential members of his congregation. Below are the stories of the members of four households in the Willard's Boundary development – households that are typical of the diverse audience Stan is trying to reach.

Heesun and Jon Kim:

Heesun Kim and her husband, Jon, moved to the U.S. from Korea seven years ago. They both grew up in Seoul, attended the National University and were married after graduation. Their backgrounds are quite similar and are typical of most Koreans. Jon's father was a small businessman (owned a small grocery store) and his wife stayed at home to tend their two children. Heesun's father was a teacher and her mother also stayed home to take care of the house and her three children.

Jon wanted to come to the U.S. to attend medical school and Heesun decided to pursue a graduate degree. When they arrived in Madison, Wisconsin, they were able to live in graduate student housing where they knew several other Korean couples. But they realized that they are in the U.S. and must also start to make friends among Americans. So, they joined a local

Methodist church (both had grown up in Christian households) which had a large percentage of Korean congregants, but also included many Americans.

Although their daughter, Hunjun was born soon after moving to Madison, Heesun continued her studies and got a Ph.D. in chemistry. When Jon finished medical school, he chose to do his residency in a Midwest community where Heesun could also find a faculty job.

When they moved, they settled in Willard's Boundary. Because their daughter is now five years old, they are anxious to put down roots and become members of the local community. That's why they are interested in attending a local church from which they received a flyer. However, they are very concerned about the impact on their daughter.

Even though they are committed to the U.S., they do not want to completely lose their heritage. They are both shy individuals who believe in discipline of the individual and children and getting ahead through education and hard work. They are appalled by the behavior they observe among many American children who do not seem to respect their parents.

Although they both work, their role behavior more closely resembles that of Koreans than liberated American couples. The house and childcare responsibilities are Heesun's because of her role obligations as wife and mother. Accentuating that are the long hours that Jon works. Frequently he is on call and not at home at night or the weekends.

Dawn Bowen and daughters

Dawn Bowen also lives in Willard's Boundary like the Kims, but her story is entirely different. She grew up in a smaller town about twenty miles away; attended the local Methodist church every Sunday and was active in the Youth Organization. She attended the local college and, upon graduation, married a man who was Roman Catholic.

They moved to Virginia Beach because he was in the Navy, and their son, Terry, was born there within nine months. The marriage had gotten off to a shaky start and crumpled within two years.

At that point, Dawn took courses at a local college to get a teaching license and began teaching language arts in the local high school. Six years later, she met a commercial airline pilot and they were soon married. Within four years, they had two daughters. When the children were born, Dawn quit work to become a full-time mother and homemaker, which she preferred to being a career woman. Her second husband was not very religious and they never attended church. After ten years, that marriage ended.

After her second divorce, Dawn decided that Virginia Beach was not working out for her and chose to move home. Her father had died four years earlier and she wanted to be closer to her mother, but not too close. So, she chose not to live in the same town.

By exhausting her marriage settlement, she was able to buy a house in the Willard's Boundary. It was convenient to school for her two middle-school-aged daughters and she liked the style of the houses. At present, she is working temporary jobs while trying to decide on a career as she is not interested in teaching again. She realizes that she must settle on something soon in order to keep up her standard of living.

Recently, she got a flyer from a local Methodist church, which grabbed her attention. She thinks that she should go to church – mostly because her mother thinks she should. There are other reasons, however. She believes it would be a good way for her daughters to meet other children their age and more importantly, she (Dawn) might meet a "better"man with whom she could have a lasting relationship.

Altice and James Rowe

Altice and James S. are an African-American couple who moved to Willard's Boundary two years ago. Altice is from Chicago and attended U. of Illinois at Chicago Circle. After graduation, she went to work for a company that makes building materials. Eventually she had to relocate in a smaller city where she met James, who is an assistant manager of a grocery store for a large Midwestern chain.

Altice is very ambitious – primarily because she wants to avoid being like her mother who dropped out of school to marry; had five children and was widowed within twelve years at the age of 29. All her life, Altice remembers monetary difficulties. Although her mother worked two jobs and she always had clothes, a roof over her head and food to eat, Altice felt deprived. She never had the same brand name clothes as the other children, she slept in a room with her four siblings and as the oldest child, she had to help take care of the younger children. University was a welcome escape for her and she paid for itself herself through student loans, a small scholarship and working part-time as a bookkeeper at a construction company.

Altice is very attracted by James' large, warm, caring family. He is one of six children – all of whom are very close and frequently get together with one another and with their parents, aunts, uncles and cousins. Altice never had a strong family support group. Because she and James are thinking about starting a family, they are concerned about the home that their children will grow up in. They both want it to be a warm, loving Christian home very much like James' parents home.

His family is made up of devout churchgoers who expect Altice and James to attend the Methodist church. While he was growing up, the church was the major social center in James life. His friends and cousins went there and his family rarely missed any Sunday services or mid-week services. All members of his family were active in the church in some way. James played softball for six years for his church in a church-sponsored softball league and the whole family came to cheer. That is how they spent most of their weekend afternoons.

Gloria and Greg Carlyle

Gloria and Greg moved to Willard's Boundary three weeks ago and are actively seeking a Methodist Church. They grew up in Alabama, attended Auburn where Gloria majored in counseling and Greg in mechanical engineering. He has worked for a local engineering firm for eight years and she works at the local community college.

They both grew up in church-going homes and have never really considered not going to church. It is their recent move that is causing them to choose a new church. They were brought up to accept the minister's word and to revere the Bible as sacred and a guide for life. Because they grew up in a blue-collar background in Birmingham, they are very industrious and ambitious – anxious to better themselves. Their new home is full of the latest electronics and they recently bought a Mercedes, which they see as the ultimate in status. They have never traveled very much, tend to be homebodies, and watch television to pass the evenings. They like to spend their time in pursuits such as playing softball, working on the lawn, and taking short day trips to local attractions whether those are state parks or theme parks.

Their only child, Bradford, will be five years old next fall, and they moved to Willard's Boundary because it is in the best school district. In addition, there is an after-school program that they think will be good for him because it contains an active sports program.

Questions for Discussion

1. What were the motivations of Stan and the pioneers in starting St. Timothy's?
2. What are the motivations of each of the four households in considering church membership?
3. Use the list of values that you found in the mission/values statement and construct a table in which the values are on the rows and the columns consist of what values you perceive for each of the following:
   a. Stan
   b. The pioneers of the church
   c. Heesun and Jon
   d. Dawn
   e. Altice and James
   f. Gloria and Greg

You could also try this exercise using typical U.S. values given in your textbook.

4. What values are imbedded in the vision/mission statement of St. Timothy's? How do these compare with typical U.S. values? *
5. Using Stan's definition of traditional, liberal and conservative, how would you characterize each of those households?
6. Using the table that you constructed in question 2 and your answers to questions 3 and 4, which households do you think will be attracted to St. Timothy's and why?
7. Which of these households would be most compatible in an adult study group together?
8. These households were chosen to represent some of the major subcultural groups in our society. Heesun and Jon are Asian American; Altice and James are African American and Dawn's household represents both divorce and blended households (children from different fathers, in this case). How do these households compare with descriptions in your textbook of these subcultures/minorities?
9. The case refers to the continuing controversy over the marketing of religion and clearly Stan is interested in "marketing his church" even if he does it in a low-key fashion. How do you feel about this? In your opinion is marketing of religion in general appropriate? Is marketing as Stan and the pioneers are doing it appropriate?
10. What changes could Stan make to attract more people to his church? (Hint: Use the research results.)

References

------, "Interview with George Barna--The Man who brought Marketing to the Church," <u>Christianity Today</u>, 1995, p. 10.

-----, "Survey of United Methodist Opinion," <u>United Methodist News Service</u>, May 1994, p. 5.

-----, "The 'Unchurched' Stuff," <u>Leadership</u>, Vol. 10, #1, p. 9.

Bradley, Martin B., Norman M. Green Jr., Dale E. Jones, Mac Lynn and Lou McNeill, <u>Churches and Church Membership in the U. S.</u>, Glenmary Research Center, Atlanta, GA. 1992

Jain, Subhash C., <u>Marketing Planning & Strategy</u>, Fourth Edition, South-Western Publishing Co., Cincinnati, Ohio, 1993.

Quinn, Bernard, Herman Andereson, Martin Bradley, Paul Goetting and Peggy Shriver, <u>Churches and Church Membership in the U. S.</u>, Glenmary Research Center, Atlanta, GA. 1982.

Warner, Fara, "Churches Develop Marketing Campaigns," <u>Wall Street Journal</u>, April 17, 1995, p. B4.

Table 1

Attendance at St. Timothy's

Date	# attending	# guests	offering
Dec. 4	150	59	$ 1,194.31
Dec. 11	132	30	726.00
Dec. 18	54	--	126.54
Dec. 25	0	--	323.25
Jan. 1	43	18	213.50
Jan. 8	115	43	477.00
Jan. 15	99	34	530.35
Jan. 22	83	22	511.00
Jan. 29	63 (ice)	17	1,522.00
Feb. 5	85	38	685.00
Feb. 12	90	32	665.40
Feb. 19	75	24	743.00
Feb. 26	76	28	1,034.67
March 5	95	29	921.96
March 12	95	33	451.00
March 19	105	32	974.00
March 26,	60	23	374.00
April 2	120	39	894.00
April 9	74	11	626.00
April 16	106	24	1,262.25
April 23	97	24	637.00
April 30	68	16	936.50
May 7	65	19	601.30
Total	2000	1301	$16,429.05

Exhibit 1

Vision/Mission Guidelines

1. Commitment and dedication to Saint Timothy's

2. Sense of self-discipline: start and end meetings on time, agenda

3. Shared responsibility/leadership

4. Consensus with prayer

5. Seek out and respect diversity; recognize and value gifts

6. Take risks, dream dreams

7. Be open to new people

8. Get all ideas out

9. Listen to all ideas

10. Value each other and commit to making the group this way

11. Begin with prayer/worship

Table 2

"Competing" Churches in the Area

Name of Church	Membership	Worship	Conducts Mailings	Telephone Contacts	Type of Church
Boundary Baptist	550	350	Subscribes To a service	No	Conservative
Willard's Boundary Community Church	200		Direct Mailings	No	Conservative
Jamestown United Methodist	1650	570	--	--	Traditional
Jamestown Episcopal	650	400	No	No	Liberal
Lutheran Church	--	--	Yes	--	Conservative

Exhibit 2

Text of Invitation to First Service

You are invited to join us as we remember the ancient story
of the birth of Jesus Christ.
We will celebrate the birth of a new community of his people,
Saint Timothy's United Methodist Church,
on

December 4

10:30 Fellowship and Refreshments
11:00 Worship

Saint Timothy's worships in the Medlin Building on the
Parkersburg Road Campus of the Parkersburg Community College.

Exhibit 3

Student Questionnaire

MBAs Need Your Help!

As part of a class project in Marketing Research, we are surveying local church members about their motivations for attending church. Please take a few minutes after the service today to complete this *anonymous* survey. Your responses will be totally confidential.

Class Representatives will collect the surveys upon your exit. Thanks for your support!

1. For the service you attended today, are you: _____ a member _____ a visitor?

2. In general, what reasons are most important to you for attending church? (Please check up to *three*.)

_____ Right way to live   _____ Overall Spirituality
_____ Important for raising my children   _____ Fellowship
_____ Part of my upbringing   _____ Salvation
_____ Other – Please specify   _____

3. Churches have different types of services, programs, pastors, even music. Please rate how important each of the following is to you, personally, using the scale below.

	Not at all Important 1	Somewhat Important 2	Very Important 3
Worship Service	_____	_____	_____
Sunday School	_____	_____	_____
Youth Program	_____	_____	_____
Adult Program	_____	_____	_____
Pastor's Skills	_____	_____	_____
Music	_____	_____	_____

Other : _____
       (Please specify.)

4. From your experience, please rate your satisfaction with the church you are attending today along those same areas.

	Not at all Important 1	Somewhat Important 2	Very Important 3
Worship Service	_____	_____	_____
Sunday School	_____	_____	_____
Youth Program	_____	_____	_____
Adult Program	_____	_____	_____
Pastor's Skills	_____	_____	_____
Music	_____	_____	_____

Other : _____
       (Please specify.)

OVER

5. How did you hear about the church you're attending today> (Check all that apply.)

_____ Mailing	_____ Word of Mouth
_____ Phone Call	_____ Drove By/Saw Sign
_____ Pastor	_____ Newspaper Advertisement
_____ Community Newsletter	_____ Other _____

(Please specify.)

6. Are you married?   _____ Yes   _____ No

7. Please check the range in which your age falls:

_____ 0 – 17 _____ 18-34 _____ 35-49 _____ 50-64 _____ 65 +

8. Please indicate the number and ages of children in your household

# of Children	Age Range
_____	0 - 2
_____	3 – 6
_____	7 – 12
_____	13 – 18
_____	19 and Over
_____	No children in household

Thank you for your help with our research project – we appreciate your support!

Table 3

Frequencies for Questions on In-Church Survey

Question 1: Membership

Answer	Frequency	Percent of Respondents
Yes	31	67.4
No	15	32.6

Question 2:   Reasons for Attending Church

Answer	Frequency	Percent of Respondents
Right Way to Live	15	32.6
Important for Raising Children	17	37.0
Part of my Upbringing	12	26.1
Overall Spirituality	35	76.1
Fellowship	38	82.6
Salvation	6	13.0

Question 3: Importance of Various Church Services

Type of Service	Not at all Important	Somewhat Important	Very Important
Worship		4	42
Sunday School		15	30
Youth Program	2	12	26
Adult Program		17	29
Pastor's Skills		6	39
Music	1	16	29
Other			7

Question 4: Satisfaction with St. Timothy's

Type of Service	Not at all Satisfied	Somewhat Satisfied	Very Satisfied
Worship		4	41
Sunday School	1	13	24
Youth Program	1	10	19
Adult Program		10	29
Pastor's Skills		3	42
Music	1	9	34
Other			4

Table 3 Cont'd.

Question 5: How did you hear about the church?

Answer	Frequency	Percent of Respondents
Mailing	11	23.9
Telephone	2	4.3
Pastor	15	32.6
Community Newsletter	4	8.7
Word of Mouth	17	37.0
Drove By/Saw Sign	1	2.2
Newspaper Ad	0	0.0
Other	10	21.7

Question 6: Marital Status

Answer	Frequency	Percent of Respondents
Single	10	21.7
Married	36	78.3

Question 7: Age Ranges of Children

Answer	Frequency	Percent of Respondents
18-34	2	17.4
35-49	24	52.2
50-64	13	28.3
65 +	1	2.2

Question 8: Number of Children and their Ages

Age Range	1 in Household	2 in Household
0- 2 years	3	2
3- 6 years	10	0
7-12 years	10	4
13-18 years	3	0
19+ years	1	3

Body Scanning: The Technology of Fit or the Fit of Technology

Fifty to sixty percent of Americans can't buy clothes that fit. Take my son for example. He's 6'5" tall, and if he buys a shirt that fits in the collar, the sleeves are too short. Obviously, anyone with his neck size is supposed to be shorter. So, what does he do? Buy shirts at the Gap and wear them with the sleeves rolled up. He's a scientific researcher, so that's all right for him. But if he were a banker, that wouldn't work. Shirt cuffs are supposed to show below the sleeves of those banker's suits.

Actually, more women than men think their clothes don't fit. They have trouble with widths because a size 10 from one manufacturer may not be the same as a size 10 from another. Actually, there is *such* disparity in sizes at most retailers that Lands' End can capitalize on the fact that all of their manufacturers make the same sizes. That means that a ten in one manufacturer's output is the same as a 10 in another one's as long as the garments are made for Lands' End.

For us tall women (I'm 6 feet tall) and for short women, length is a major issue. The tall women are mostly out of luck as it's difficult to lengthen garments. The short women can sometimes find Petites, but the selection is limited. Sometimes garments can be shortened but the waist, hip or bust line may still be in the wrong place. Or maybe they can shop in the Juniors section. When you're 40, the Juniors section isn't the right look – especially for professional clothing. Then, of course there are separate issues for people who are overweight.

Fit has become such a big issue that companies like Levi's are taking action about it. In the past, Levi's offered us jeans adjusted to fit if you sent them your measurements. Actually, Levi's made jeans in several different versions for each size and the company sent you the one that most closely matched your measurements. In other words, the jeans were not made individually for the purchaser. But that is changing. Recently, Levi's devoted a section of its new flagship store in San Francisco to customization services.

A major component of these services is a body scanner made by TC^2 – a textile research company whose full name is Textile/Clothing Technology Corporation. The purpose of the body scanner is to produce accurate body measurements by producing an image of your body based on over 100,000 measurements taken by several cameras connected to a computer. (To see what these images and scans look like, visit the TC Squared web site at http://www.TC2.com.)

To be scanned, you enter a changing room; take off your clothes and don stretchable jockey-type underwear (nothing that crimps or compresses the body, such as a girdle); then step into a black booth; stand on the white footprints on the floor; grab the hand rails; close your eyes and stand perfectly still for 12-15 seconds while white lights flash and the computer captures the images. By the time you are dressed, the computer has produced a black image scan for you. Using the data captured in the scan, a sales associate at Levi's can help you select clothing using your body scan measurements as a guide. Or, you can have virtual try-ons by fitting various garments on the scanned image in the computer. If you find something you like, you can then try on the real thing. Simple, right?

The whole process can take less than twenty minutes from the decision to try the scanning technology to finding (virtually) a new outfit that should fit almost perfectly. If what you want is not quite right, Levi's will alter it for you. This eliminates a lot of the hassle in shopping. No more going into the changing room with 10 articles of clothing only to find that three or four don't fit (too big, short, long, tight, etc.)

Through numerous tests, TC^2 found that scanned measurements are much more accurate than measurements made by hand – even measurements made by professional tailors. One would think that the promise of perfect fitting clothes would have consumers knocking down the doors for $TC^{2's}$ technology, but that has not proved to be the case. Why?

First of all, there's a question of where and under what conditions would you be scanned. Should scanners be located in stores such as Levi's (belong to retailers) or be free-standing units in malls? If the latter, then who owns the scanner? TC^2 is a research firm without the resources to maintain scanners at malls across the U.S. Until the scanners prove to be either profitable or real traffic-builders, mall companies are reluctant to invest in them. If they did, they would have to staff and maintain them.

Second, there's a question of what happens to the data? Once you've been scanned, would you want to think that your measurements (along with your name) are floating around in a database somewhere? Of course, you could walk away with your scan and your measurements on a smart card, but then how would you communicate them to a manufacturer to order clothing? At the Levi's store, the company is saving the scanned measurements in a database that it can use in sizing research to determine the appropriate shapes and sizes of garments in the future and giving you a paper copy to keep.

Third, there's a question of what you would do with your measurements after you get them. Ideally, you would want to order custom-made clothes, but who would you order them from? Levi's possibly. There are very few manufacturers ready to receive your scanned measurements at present and even when you find those, transmitting the data requires special equipment. If the scanners are in stores other than Levi's (and TC^2 will be placing scanners in a few stores), then you can use the data to virtually shop that store's inventory to find what is most likely to fit you. But you could only shop that store's inventory. You couldn't use the data at a store down the street or elsewhere in the mall unless those stores have the sizes and measurements of their inventories in computerized databases.

Using the data from store to store requires cooperation among retailers which raises the question of why should one store buy the scanner and then share the data with other stores? Also, it means that retailers must put the sizes and measurements of its inventories into readily accessible computer bases. This would require measuring of garments as they do not always come with measurements pre-specified. Also, the retailer would have to invest in computers and/or terminals that consumers could use. It's a lot more work for the retailer with little demonstrable return at present. In all of these "solutions" there's a need for information transmission between retailers and manufacturers that does not exist at present.

Fourth, if you gain/lose weight or if you grow taller, the measurements are invalid. You would have to be scanned again. Compared to other problems in the introduction of this technology, this one seems minor, but still very real.

All along TC^2 has known that selling the scanners will be difficult. They not only faced the problems outlined previously, but also had to deal with issues of cost and size. Initially, they were around $200,000 but the price has gradually come down to less than $75,000. They also took up a lot of floor space – more than four to six changing rooms, but TC^2 has slimmed the booths down to not much more space than two large changing rooms. Scanner space needs have gone from around 100 square feet to 50 square feet.

While that doesn't sound like much, it's square footage that doesn't directly contribute to sales. All retailers are interested in their sales and profits per square foot in the store. Thus, their goal is to maximize the amount of selling square footage to non-selling square footage. Scanners would increase the amount of non-selling square footage.

To better understand consumer attitudes toward scanning, TC^2 cooperated with a local university research project in which 49 students volunteered to be scanned. Of those 49 students, 68% had problems buying clothes (so they are similar to the U.S. population). Their reasons for being scanned were to obtain exact body measurements (41%), curiosity (34%) and to get better fitting clothes (24%). After going through the scanning procedure, 98% preferred the scanning process to physical measurement with a tape measure. Their reasons were: more accurate (43%), easier (14%), quicker (25%), less physical contact (16%) and it's new (2%). Respondent attitudes toward the body scanning experience are shown in Table 1. 48 of the 49 students said they would go through the scanning experience again.

How did the experience differ from their expectations? It was faster (33%); easier (5%); fun and exciting (10%); and wasn't invasive (3%). On the other hand, one person had expected a photograph rather than an image; another found standing still difficult and two had not expected to have to strip for the scanning. What did they like most? It measured biceps (2%), the flashing lights (6%), seeing one's self in 3-D (26%), speed and accuracy (23%), easier than physical measurement (2%), new and fun (15%), took a short time (4%) and lights and music (6%).

Table 1

Attitude Scores of Respondents

Attitudinal Statement	Strongly Disagree	Disagree	Neutral	Agree	Strongly Agree
The body scanning experience was fun and interesting.	4.26	0.00	8.51	17.02	70.21
The body scanning experience was scary.	48.94	23.40	2.13	4.26	4.26
The body scanning experience was exciting	2.13	2.13	17.02	23.40	55.32
The body scanning experience was bothersome.	56.52	23.91	15.22	0.00	4.35

What did they like least? The long wait (7%), cold temperature (9%), the underwear that had to be worn (9%), the physical measuring process (13% – this was for comparison), the music played during the scan (4% – this was music from the movie Pretty Woman), strangers seeing them in a leotard (2%), computer errors (2%), filling out the survey (4%) and the lack of clear body landmarks (2%). On the other hand, 44% found nothing to dislike in the process.   By the way, one gets to keep the underwear to re-assure consumers that they are not putting on "used" underwear.

Naturally, TC^2 asked what people would pay for body scanning. Believe it or not, 11% said they would pay more than 75$; 19% would pay $51-75; 23% would pay $26-50; and 25% would pay $10 - $25. The average price that males would be willing to pay for scanning was $46 and females would pay $37.

All respondents would recommend body scanning to others. Their advice to others would be that this is good if you want custom or better fitting clothes, (17%), worthwhile (15%), measurements are more accurate (4%), and it's fascinating, fun, efficient, quick and easy (35%).

Where did they think that body scanning should be offered? 33% thought it should be available at central mall locations; 29% at department stores; 35% at specialty stores and 3% at a free-standing location.

Of the participants, 98% said they would order custom clothing using the scanned measurements. Their reasons were better fit (40%), more accurate (15%), perfect clothes (20%), tailored fit (12.5%), and to get clothes long enough (5 %). The one person who would not order custom clothing gave expense as the reason.

On the issue of expense: One normally thinks of custom clothing as more expensive, but that need not be the case. Consider that in the channel of distribution, both the manufacturer and retailer bear the costs of clothes that don't sell in the form of markdowns and returns. If all clothes were custom-ordered and made, then there would be less waste, smaller inventories and everyone could survive on lower margins. Of course, we are not likely to reach a point at which all clothes are custom-made, but knowing that retailers and manufacturers could use more efficient inventory control, smaller inventories and reduce costs of waste, returns and markdowns indicates that custom clothes need not be much more expensive. How much would you pay to get perfect fitting suits? Slacks? Dresses? Evening wear?   Would you pay 10%, 20%?

The ability of the productive/distributive system to get Jane and Joe Doe custom tailored clothing through the mass marketing system is called mass customization. Mass customization is already with us on the Internet. Many of us have personal pages at services such as Yahoo (My Yahoo), Amazon (My Amazon) and other Internet sites where we have custom ordered information. We have mass customization of services such as cell phones, banking services, insurance, financial plans, etc. Companies can produce mass customized mailings. Both General Motors and Honda have toyed with mass customization of autos (Yep, you order your own, customized Saturn or Accord.). Because mass customization can reduce waste and risk for the manufacturer and retailer as well as customized product offerings to consumers, it has advantages for everyone.

While the university research results seem to be very encouraging, remember that these are college students volunteering for an experiment. At the end of the process, they could not really order clothes. Thus, it is difficult to extrapolate from these results to the general population.

A survey by Kurt Salmon and Associates sheds light on how the larger population feels about body scanning. It revealed that 66% of the population was comfortable with having their body scanned; 59% said they would use it if it is available; 60% had difficulty with finding well-fitting clothes; 18% would pay for body scanning and 36% would pay more for custom-made clothes. Only 29% of their respondents were satisfied with the fit of currently available clothing. Not bad considering that the respondents only had descriptions of the body scanning technology, not actual experience with it.

After thinking through the problems of introducing the technology for several years, TC^2 decided that a catalog company would be a good way to introduce the benefits of body scanning to the public. Customers who had been scanned could send their measurements to the cataloger who could in turn send them to the appropriate producer of the desired clothing.

What cataloger would make a good partner for the scanner? What about Lands' End which had already dived into the fit-issue waters with My Virtual Model. Through the Virtual Model, consumers could build their own model (including skin tones, hair color and shape of eyes) on which they could then try on various outfits sold by Lands' End. By combining with TC^2, Lands' End could offer their customers more precise fittings by using scanning data to adjust garments to the Virtual Model.

Using the name, ImageTwin, TC^2 and a partner teamed up with Lands' End for the *Lands' End My Virtual Model Tour* in the fall of 2000.   By putting the scanning booth and equipment inside an eighteen-wheeler, the Virtual Tour hit the road for 14 U.S. cities between October and December.

Lands' End was one of the first catalog companies to invest heavily in the Internet. Early on, it put its entire catalog and other features on the Internet and pioneered security features to entice consumers to order online. Recognizing that consumers are most concerned about improper fit and the hassle of returning clothes, it is not surprising that this company believes that online customer service is crucial and can be enhanced through tools such as body scanning and virtual try-ons.   Indeed, adding these tools helped Lands' End be named a "gold standard" for customer online service by *Business Week* magazine and to be inducted into the *Smithsonian* for outstanding achievements in leading the information technology revolution to enhance and enable the relationship between company and customer.

How do consumers feel about the use of these new tools? While the tour was in New York City, a reporter for the Wall Street Journal took advantage of the opportunity to be scanned. She was negative about the experience because it was cold, she didn't like the underwear she was given, she was rushed through the scan, the scan had to be re-done because her hair had fallen down (it must be pinned to the top of one's head during the scan) although she could not find any hair that had fallen, the assistant came into the booth to help her with her hair and the computer measured her hips much wider than she thought they were. Afterwards, she measured herself and had a tailor measure her and both measurements found her hips to be smaller than the computer measurements. After complaining to Lands' End, she finally got an acknowledgement that the computer models were way too "hippy." So, computers can make imaging mistakes. A side issue is where does one measure hips. The TC^2 scanner may measure at a different location than do tailors and that can account for differences in the measurements.

The reporter's experience highlights a crucial issue for TC^2. Many consumers have images of themselves and the size they wear. Information to the contrary is not welcome. Few of us are totally satisfied with our bodies and therefore pictures and images that do not correspond with our image may be rejected.

Furthermore, fit is not a straightforward matter. Researchers at the TC^2 facility have watched consumers come out of the scanning booth and, by use of the computer, try on jeans. Some consumers want those jeans skintight and others want them baggy. But all consumers might say that the jeans they select "fit." Sometimes people select jeans with a 1.5 inch negative waist easement. What does that mean? The jeans measure 1.5 inches less than the person's waist. That is more than skintight! Pains me just to think about it.

Thus, fit is more than a matter of standardizing all size tens to measure the same. It's also a reflection of the consumers' preferences and comfort levels. It's also a matter of style as some styles can lend themselves to being worn skintight while others can only be worn loosely. It's also a matter of fabric. Stretchy fabrics are more comfortable when worn skintight. And it can be a matter of occasion. One might wear clothes with a relaxed fit for gardening, sports or lounging around, but want a tighter fit for more formal, dressy occasions.

Where does TC^2 go from here in convincing consumers to use body scanning? At present, they have hooked up with Brooks Brothers to put a scanner in their New York store so that Brooks Brothers can be mass customizing suits and shirts at no extra charge using the computer generated images. In addition, consumers in the Raleigh, NC area can be scanned locally at a mall or at the TC^2 facilities and order clothes from Brooks Brothers.

One resident who recently took advantage of this opportunity was Dick Gurley, who is short and stocky. His shirts are usually too long in the sleeves and neck and have to be altered. Using his measurements from the scanning experience, he ordered a blue shirt with white collar and cuffs that fit "absolutely perfectly." "It was amazing," he said. At last, shirts that fit!

One might question the wisdom of teaming with Brooks Brothers in an era of business casual, but that era may be changing. According to a Wall Street Journal article, business people are starting to dress up more. President Bush has been instrumental in changing business clothing standards as he requires jackets and ties and no jeans – even on weekends. But this trend does not stop and start at the White House. Some companies have found that "business casual" is interpreted by some employees as "business sloppy" and have set more business-appropriate apparel standards. Also, many unemployed dot-comers looking for more traditional jobs find that the jeans and polo shirt casual approach does not work in job interviews. Finally, some employees just feel better in business suits and ties. One Atlanta customer who had ordered four custom-made suits says he feels more professional when dressed up. Thus, Brooks might make a good partner for TC^2 given that they have traditionally sold clothing that customers custom ordered or had altered for more formal occasions that merit extra expenditure and which seem to be on the rebound. Brooks Brothers is high end and their customers are already prepared to pay more.

Another outlet for body scanners is specialty stores such as the Body Print, a boutique opened in Atlanta in May 2001. This specialty shop makes custom clothes for consumers – everything from slacks to bridesmaid dresses. Bring your own designs or select one of theirs. Again, this shop is selling items that consumers have probably decided to spend extra for. While this is encouraging for TC^2, the number of these outlets is small compared to the all other retailers.

This has led TC^2 to consider other markets for their scanners. One such market might be health centers. Body scanning enables one to measure muscle mass evenly throughout the body (as well as fat). Thus, body builders find it a useful technique for tracking their progress over time.

Other markets include uniforms. Think of the U.S. military's need for uniforms. Does it make sense for the Army, Navy, Marines, Air Force and Coast Guard to stockpile thousands of uniforms to dole out to officers and enlisted persons? Or would it make more sense to scan personnel and order uniforms to fit so that all military personnel would have uniforms that are long enough or short enough and the right width around.

Another uniform market is for companies such as UPS or FedEx or the U.S. Postal service. All their employees wear uniforms that help to identify and promote their services. Again, it might be less costly and more efficient to have custom-made suits rather than stockpiling lots of sizes. After all, the purpose of uniforms is to produce a professional look. Is it professional if the pants and sleeves aren't long enough?

Some scanner producers have focused exclusively on the uniform market, especially the military uniform market, but TC^2 recognizes that the larger market is the final consumer or retail market.

The consumer market, however, is not limited to the U.S. Retailers and even governments in other countries have shown an interest in standardizing styles.

In the U.K., leading British retailers such as Marks & Spencer and Bhs PLC, Next, C&A, and Sears Clothing are teaming with universities and the government to sponsor a national sizing survey to measure 20,000 to 30,000 women, men and children. The goal is to develop a three-dimensional body-measurement system that would ultimately let shoppers try clothes on computer-generated replicas of themselves. This program will result in the creation of an U.K. Center for 3D Electronic Commerce to be part of University College, London. The U.K. Department of Trade and Industry is providing $2 million toward the cost of this project in order to develop demonstration scanners, in-store kiosks, Internet services and interactive television links – all of which have to be developed within an eighteen month period that ends near the end of 2001.

Part of the reason for this research is the same as in the U.S. It's to standardize sizes – at least in the U.K. Anyone who has ever shopped in Europe knows that there's vast differences between U.S. and European sizes. Thus, standardizing sizes on a country basis might be the first step toward global, standardized sizing which would make shopping around the globe much easier than it is at present. It might also make manufacturing of garments easier as well.

The U.K. research model is intriguing because it includes government support and a coalition of retailers. The folks at TC^2 think that retailers are the key to unlocking the potential of body scanning. They are the gateway to the market for manufacturers and the provider of supply for consumers. Thus, their position in the middle of the channel between the consumer and manufacturer enhances their ability to broker changes and speed up/slow down the adoption of changes in the channel. If retailers demanded custom-made clothes, manufacturers would probably fall into line, but there's little reason for retailers to demand this until the consumer does. Thus, stimulating consumer demand is a major goal of TC^2. The involvement of government provides an infusion of needed cash to stimulate the diffusion of these electronic innovations.

Is TC^2 part of the British study? You betcha'. They've sold scanners to those researchers and they're hoping that the success of scanning technology in the U.K. will lead to greater interest in the U.S. and speedier adoption of this technology in the U.S.

If this catches on, how well will TC^2's scanner do in the marketplace? At present, there are six competitors in this market. Two are located in the U.S., and one each are found in Germany, France, the U.K. and Japan. The main difference between scanners is the technology they employ. The German and one U.S.-made scanner use lasers and the Japanese scanner uses Infra red technology. TC^2 chose white light technology because it is safer (as long as you keep your eyes closed during the scanning) than lasers. Actually, the danger to the eyes is minimal. Even if you leave your eyes open, you'll just see lots and lots of dancing dots in front of your eyes after the scan rather than real eye damage. All scanners take about the same time to process (10 – 17 seconds) except the French Scanner which takes one second. The TC^2 Scanner has no moving parts, fits within 50 sq. feet and takes robust body measurements. While most of the other scanners fit within approximately the same area, they take far fewer measurements and some have moving parts such as steps. Thus, the TC^2 scanner offers the most in terms of measurements and safety of the scanners on the market – features that the developers built into the design.

So TC^2 is ready with this technology; the British are moving toward a working model of 3D electronic commerce; a few U.S. retailers are using the technology, but progress in the U.S. is still slow. In the meantime, I guess my son and I will have to make do with what we can find in the tall shop *if* we can find a tall shop. But it's dispiriting to know that the UPS person is going to be walking around in better fitting clothes than I can buy.

Questions for Discussion

1. What need(s) does body scanning fill? Are these likely to be highly motivating to consumers?
2. What are the risks that consumers perceive in body scanning? How could TC^2 deal with these?
3. Body Scanning is an innovation. How does it rate on the characteristics of an innovation that determine the rate of adoption? (relative advantage, trialability, compatibility, observability and communicability)
4. How could TC^2 attempt to overcome any problems identified in Question 2?
5. What are the advantages of body scanning for the consumer? Clothing retailers? Clothing manufacturers? Is there a real advantage?
6. What are the disadvantages to consumers? Clothing retailers? Clothing manufacturers?
7. How can the issue of fit be dealt with? Is this a rational or emotional issue?
8. Can you think of other markets that might use body scanning technology?
9. Try designing promotional materials for body scanning that would be aimed at the consumer market. What would you tell consumers? (How could you use the data from the surveys in the case?)
10. In your opinion, what is the best means of introducing body scanning technology to the clothing market? Is it through free standing mall locations, at major retailers, catalogers or through specialty shops?

References

Agins, Teri, "Head Up-the Suits are Coming," Wall Street Journal, April 6, 2001, p. B1 & B4.

DesMarteau, Kathleen, "Leading the Way in Changing Times," Bobbin, October 1999.

D'Innocenzio, Anne, "Try Scan on for Size," Chicago Sun-Times, October 19, 2000, p 5.

Fallon, James, "British Retailers Kick off Body-Scanning Project," Daily News Record, Feb. 10, 1999, p. 13.

Holme, Beverly, "Lands' End Introduces Latest Online Shopping Innovations: Setting New E-commerce Standards for Customer Service," Lands' End Press Releases, Fall 2000.

Quick, Rebecca, "Getting the Right Fit – Hips and All," Wall Street Journal, October 18, 2000, p. B1B4.

Silverman, Dick, "Altered States – A Better Fit through Body Scanning," WWD, Nov. 11, 1998, p. 8.

Wellington, Elizabeth," For good Measure," <u>Raleigh News and Observer</u>, December, 5, 2000, 1E & 3E.